A
HISTORY of
Connecticut
FOOD

A HISTORY of
Connecticut
FOOD

*A Proud Tradition of Puddings, Clambakes
and Steamed Cheeseburgers*

ERIC D. LEHMAN & AMY NAWROCKI

Charleston · London

THE
History
PRESS

Published by The History Press
Charleston, SC 29403
www.historypress.net

Copyright © 2012 by Eric D. Lehman and Amy Nawrocki
All rights reserved

Cover Images courtesy of Holmberg Orchards, Frank Pepe's Pizzeria,
Jeff Kaufman (Match Restaurant) and the authors.

First published 2012

Manufactured in the United States

ISBN 978.1.60949.512.1

Library of Congress CIP data applied for.

HUNGER

What if the egg
never cracked or the slick moon
of a spoon never borrowed broth
from the blackened kettle
to meet our lips?

What if the apple tree
never shook in a spring storm
or a mantle of snow
never foretold future greens
and silky yellows?

If the cook never tested the pie
or the famished traveler
never asked for seconds,
whose heart would break
with meringue's collapse
or the steak's charred crust
folding toward a knife edge?

How would we nourish
our labors if not with
the earth's capacity to feed us
and the tongue's aptitude
for savoring?

How would we find
our true selves, spice and all,
without plunging hands
into a mound of dough
or stealing a lick with sloppy fingers?

Who will butter our bread
if not the crepuscular calls
of hunger from which we have
happily never escaped?

Contents

CONTENTS

Introduction

In 1726, dozens of visitors from around Connecticut rushed to Stonington for the marriage of Temperance Tealleys and Reverend William Worthington. This enthusiasm probably had more to do with the anticipated feast than sentiment for the admittedly popular couple. Over the course of two days, eager guests gorged on stewed oysters, baked cornbread, fried potatoes, casseroled pumpkin and rich chowders of fish and clams. They savored steaming venison, roasted pig and crispy duck. For dessert, they ate dried-plum Indian pudding drenched in a molasses, butter and vinegar sauce or cracked off a piece of maple sugar and hickory nut candy. To wash their meals down, they drained mugs of black coffee and dipped tankards into a huge stone punch bowl, filled with native hard cider and imported sugar, lemons and limes. The feast extended to a third day when friendly Mohawks and Pequots arrived to share in the chowder and pork and in the fun and fellowship. After all, not every year was so bountiful, and surviving the lean times reminded everyone that food not only gave life but also made life worth living.

Yet by the middle of the nineteenth century, Connecticut author Harriet Beecher Stowe said of her more prosperous nation, "There is no country where an ample, well-furnished table is more easily spread, and for that reason, none where the bounties of Providence are more generally neglected." She bemoaned the fact that too many took food for granted. The same could be said of twenty-first-century Americans, though luckily in recent decades things have been changing for the better. More of us are interested in not only where the food on our plates comes from but also where food itself comes from. Why are these foods *our* foods?

That is the subject we explore in this book—part history, part instruction. Every cookbook should include the back story necessary to understand how a recipe came to work, and any history of food is incomplete without recipes. The two elements bubble together here like a pot of baked beans over an open fire, naturally leading to a greater appreciation of the food, an appreciation that helps make us human. As Madison's resident world-famous chef Jacques Pepin tells us, "The food you have at home grows on you and becomes more important than simply the food itself. It becomes associated with all parts of your life in a very deep way, part of your roots, your inner self."

Pepin is echoing the common aphorism that you are what you eat, the earliest known printed English example of which was a 1923 advertisement for beef in one of our local newspapers, the *Bridgeport Telegraph*. But that adage has transformed into a motto for healthy eating rather than what gastronome Jean Anthelme Brillat-Savarin first meant when he said something of the kind in 1826: that your choice of food is part of your spirit, a taste of the truth about you.

So, keeping in mind that the food of the past makes us who we are even as it develops into the food of the present, this history focuses on the crops, game, livestock, seafood and prepared cuisine that we have or once had a relationship with. Some of the foods will seem familiar to you and some strange, even if you've lived in the state all your life. Perhaps you did not even consider that there was such a thing as "Connecticut food" or that it deserved a place alongside the great regional foods of America. Hopefully we can open your mind and your mouth.

Of course, the food eaten by Connecticutians, or Nutmeggers, or Connectors or whatever we wish to be called, has changed with the centuries, absorbing influences from without and evolving from within. In fact, our actual taste buds have changed, and the dishes people adored three hundred years ago taste strange to us today. A bowl of Indian pudding seems bland to us, even with extra molasses. A frothy mug of flip crafted in the traditional way tastes burnt and bitter. Furthermore, some of the ingredients and methods are no longer valid or available. We are unlikely to eat seal, and certainly not the local ones. The American "pheasant," really a type of grouse, will never be on our menus, nor will the subtle delicacy of the extinct passenger pigeon, eaten with bits of salt pork, thyme and pounded biscuit. It is also unlikely that you will test your cake with a clean broom splinter or measure butter by comparing it to a hen's egg.

With that in mind, many traditional recipes have been reinterpreted, though in some cases the originals remain valid and tasty. Some would say it's hard to improve on a basic hot lobster roll or roast duck. These recipes are supplemented with instructions from some of Connecticut's finest contemporary chefs, taking classic ingredients and dishes and turning them into something sublime. We hope that the delicious recipes will inspire you to learn about our land's culinary history and vice versa. However, more than that, perhaps you will be moved to reexamine your relationship with food, with cooking and perhaps with Connecticut itself.

Hartford resident, humorist and epicure Mark Twain once said that "part of the secret of success in life is to eat what you like and let the food fight it out inside." Hopefully you'll find something you like in this book. Turn the page and take a seat at our table.

PART I

Rooted in Our Soil:
Fruits and Vegetables

1

The Well-Earned Feast

One of the most famous food poems of all time, Joel Barlow's "Hasty Pudding," was written while the author and diplomat toured Europe, pining for the savory corn mush of his Redding, Connecticut home. He writes:

> *I sing the sweets I know, the charms I feel,*
> *My morning incense, and my evening meal,*
> *The sweets of Hasty Pudding. Come, dear bowl,*
> *Glide o'er my palate, and inspire my soul.*

This attitude at the end of the eighteenth century was a huge leap forward from the first European colonists, who found corn-based dishes practically inedible. The niece of Connecticut governor John Winthrop wrote to him from Stamford in 1649, happily declaring that her generous husband ate corn so that she could eat wheat. It is not an exaggeration to say that corn, and all the other foods Native Americans ate, was considered close to sinful by the first Europeans—"tainted with savagery."

They had little choice, though, since wheat grew poorly in the rocky New England soil. Native Americans taught the colonists how to grind and cook corn, or "turkey wheat," something they likely had been doing here since the end of the last ice age. Throughout that time, corn developed into different strains and, by 1300, was being farmed intensively. The local Pequot tribe cleared small areas by burning brush, pushed up earth mounds a few feet apart with turtle shell hoes and placed corn kernels in the mounds. They sometimes planted beans, as well, allowing the vines to climb the cornstalks. In between the mounds, they planted squash. Once the crops were harvested, the Pequots moved inland to their forested winter camps.

The dishes that Native Americans made from this "super crop" were simple but effective. They often made porridge with ground corn and water, mixing in fruit, meat or nuts. Corn pounded into powder was taken on long journeys in a pouch and simply eaten in handfuls or baked in ashcakes. They also roasted ears on the fire, something that took a little longer for colonial Europeans to appreciate, though eventually it became a dietary staple. The kernels in those days were not as sweet, so charring a cob was a way of making it more appetizing.

A simple mix of corn and beans—succotash—was another popular recipe because the corn of the day lacked certain amino acids that are plentiful in beans. (A few centuries later, the Connecticut Agricultural Experiment Station would be the first to develop the amino-rich hybrid corn we eat today.) The native farmers did not have fancy Latinate words for this concept, but they understood the nutritional value of mixing the vegetables. When corn was introduced into other parts of the world without this knowledge, vitamin deficiency led to terrifying results. Building on the natives' foundations, the colonists' recipes for succotash would include husked shell beans, green beans or lima beans with onion, bacon or salt pork, fresh corn, salt, pepper and heavy cream. Some later recipes called for ripe tomatoes or nutmeg.

After just a few decades, arriving colonists were not dying of starvation in the winter forests any longer, and cultivation of crops and livestock began to increase. Samuel Wakeman, a parson in Fairfield in the mid-1600s, kept fifty sheep, pigs and cows and a beehive. His stores included honey, malt, wheat and, of course, corn. Planting took place when a ridge was formed with two furrows. Using a hoe, corn was planted at distances of four feet. If you had an ox team, you could plow an acre a day. From that acre, a farmer could expect forty bushels of corn ears. In 1652, corn was plentiful, bringing three shillings per bushel, but by 1693 this price had dropped to two shillings. By the 1700s, wheat brought from Europe had been completely abandoned as a viable crop, and corn was king. It remained the favorite, easiest and most productive crop for two hundred years.

As corn continued to be the staple fare throughout the 1700s, and with food in general more plentiful and the dangers of blights and famines lessened, corn became available for molasses production. Ezra Stiles, president of Yale College, pointed out that "this is done with only the Topping of the corn without damaging the Ear or Grain…they have already made considerable Molasses from Corn Tops and some of the Molasses has been distilled into good Rum." Edward Hinman of Stratford was given the "right" to do this as early as 1717. However, this industry became less useful later in the century with the cheap importation of molasses from the Caribbean.

By this time, no one thought of corn as unappetizing. Instead, it was a healthy and tasty part of the meal. The most common dish was Barlow's favorite "hasty pudding" or "Indian pudding." The names were sometimes used interchangeably, though a few differences do appear in the preparation. Originally, hasty pudding was a dish from England made with oatmeal or wheat and milk, but the name soon became applied solely to the corn version popularized in the Americas.

Ironically, "haste" had no part in the cooking and baking methods to create it, which in colonial times could take all day. Instead, the title probably refers to the effort taken by the cook. As Barlow writes, "Meanwhile the housewife urges all her care, / The well-earned feast to hasten and prepare."

We have definitely lost the art of cooking in "bags" or "pudding cloths" and standing all day over a slow fire, and even by the turn of the nineteenth century, the preparation for puddings of this type had become much hastier. The recipes also vary widely; Amelia Simmons, author of *American Cookery*, published in Hartford in 1796, has three versions. Some use eggs, and some do not. Some use a small amount of cornmeal and lots of milk, and some the opposite. Sometimes hasty pudding recipes incorporate just water, while Indian pudding recipes use milk or milk and water. Some suggest eating it with molasses; others suggest combining it with diced apples, raisins, ginger, cloves or cinnamon. But one thing all agree on is that "the preparation of this pudding cannot be hurried." The cornmeal needs to thicken and absorb liquid slowly or it "will be spoiled."

Although Barlow's poem includes a "recipe" for hasty pudding ("Through the rough sieve to shake the golden shower, / In boiling water stir the yellow flour"), this one from *The Early American Cookbook* is a lot easier to follow:

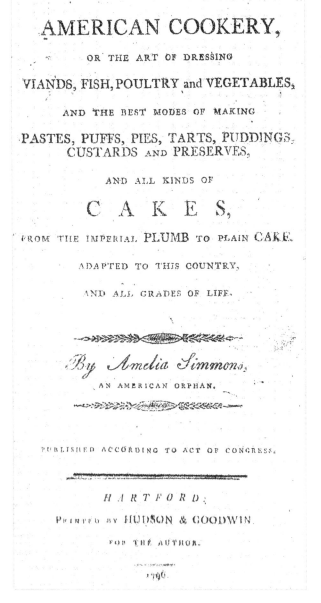

AMERICAN COOKERY,

OR THE ART OF DRESSING

VIANDS, FISH, POULTRY and VEGETABLES,

AND THE BEST MODES OF MAKING

PASTES, PUFFS, PIES, TARTS, PUDDINGS, CUSTARDS AND PRESERVES,

AND ALL KINDS OF

C A K E S,

FROM THE IMPERIAL PLUMB TO PLAIN CAKE.

ADAPTED TO THIS COUNTRY,

AND ALL GRADES OF LIFE.

By Amelia Simmons,

AN AMERICAN ORPHAN.

PUBLISHED ACCORDING TO ACT OF CONGRESS.

H A R T F O R D:

PRINTED BY HUDSON & GOODWIN.

FOR THE AUTHOR.

1796.

Published in 1796 in Hartford, Amelia Simmons's *American Cookery* was the first cookbook to catalogue the many "receipts" of the newly independent country.

Hasty Pudding
....

2½ cups water
¾ teaspoon salt
1 cup cornmeal
Sweetening of choice—molasses, sugar, honey or maple syrup
Milk or cream

Bring water and salt to a brisk boil "in a deep heavy kettle" or saucepan. Sprinkle cornmeal and whisk, stirring continuously. Reduce heat and simmer 30 minutes, stirring every few minutes. If using a double boiler, which we recommend, cook for 1 hour. Sweeten after cooking with molasses, maple syrup, sugar or honey. Serve in a bowl with milk or cream. Some like it with bacon bits or with apples, especially for breakfast.

Rye flour can also be used, especially for those with delicate stomachs. Lydia Child, in *The American Frugal Housewife*, suggests: "If the system is in a restricted state, nothing can be better than *rye* hasty pudding and *West Indian* molasses. This diet would save many a one in the horrors of dyspepsia." Another way that Indian pudding differs from the hasty sort is that, in modern times (the past two centuries), most call for the additional step of baking the boiled mush in an oven.

In the nineteenth century, Indian pudding changed from being served for breakfast or as a prelude to dinner to being eaten as a dessert. The inclusion of multiple sweeteners and additional spice, as well as the possibility of whipped cream or ice cream in recipes like the one that follows, makes the dish a considerable indulgence.

Indian Pudding
....

3½ cups hot water
3½ cups whole milk or light cream
¾ cup yellow cornmeal
3 tablespoons butter
3 eggs

¾ cup dark molasses
½ cup sugar
½ teaspoon salt
¾ teaspoon cinnamon
½ teaspoon ginger

In a double boiler, combine hot water and 2 cups milk. Make sure to use light cream or at least whole milk or the pudding will be watery. Add cornmeal slowly, whisking smooth. Cook over a light boil 15–20 minutes until thick as oatmeal. Cool slightly and add butter; stir until smooth. In another bowl, beat eggs, molasses, spices and salt. Pour into buttered baking dish and cook for 30 minutes at 350 degrees. Pour the remaining milk over top and cook for an additional 30 minutes until set. Cool and thicken for at least 30 minutes and serve with ice cream or whipped cream.

A recipe from Torrington in 1904 suggests putting layers of "boiled frosting" in between layers of the Indian pudding to make a "layer cake." It also seems that people used fewer eggs and less molasses as time went on, increasing the spices instead, probably as corn itself became sweeter and more palatable. Still, by 1900, fried Indian pudding remained a common breakfast dish. In *Connecticut Magazine*, Louise Bunch tells us to stir a quart of warm water into a pint of cornmeal gradually, stirring, boiling and adding a teacup of white flour, continuing to stir, adding more boiling water and simmering for three hours. Like all who talk of Indian pudding, she stresses slowness. Then she says to "mould in a tin brick and allow to become absolutely cold. Twenty minutes before serving, cut into thin slices and fry in very hot lard."

Of course, pudding was not the only preparation of corn, nor was ground meal the only result of harvest. Kernels, especially as corn became sweeter, were separated from the cob and cooked on their own or added to recipes for texture. A recipe for corn pudding from 1900 calls for three eggs, sixteen ounces of canned corn, two tablespoons of margarine, one-third cup of sugar, one-half cup of milk and one-half teaspoon of salt. Combine everything in a mixing bowl and pour into a greased baking dish, cooking at 350 degrees for thirty-five to forty minutes. Cookbook contributor Isabella Witt of Stonington used cream, not milk, and less sugar, while adding pepper.

"Corn oysters" were battered fritters using whole corn, spooned into an oyster-like shape, fried and eaten with honey or maple syrup. Corn cakes could also be shaped, using meal or kernels, and fried if you had a large jar of lard or fat in your pantry. If you didn't, a "Sachem's Head Corn Cake" used two cups and six tablespoons of cornmeal, six tablespoons of sugar, one-half teaspoon of salt, three cups of scalded milk, one-half teaspoon of dissolved baking soda and four eggs. The yolks, meal, salt and milk were mixed, and then the egg whites were beaten to a froth and stirred in just before "it goes to bake" until done, at 350 degrees in a modern oven.

Corn chowder was also popular, replacing clams with fresh corn kernels. Salt pork was soaked in boiling water and then crisped on high heat, using the rendering fat to sauté diced onions. Adding potatoes, stock, pepper, salt, thyme, hard crackers and optional hot milk or cream slowly, the soup would cook on low heat. Some added clams, as well, making delicious combination chowder.

Possibly the most popular method for turning corn into appealing food, however, was flapjacks. They were often called johnnycakes, a derivative of "journey cake," meaning they were easy to take on the road. According to some sources, "Johnny" was short for Connecticut's Revolutionary War governor, Jonathan Trumbull, whom General Washington credited with winning the war by feeding the Continental army. However, before they were called this, they were called slapjacks or flapjacks, and when "johnnycake" began to be used for another kind of bread in the mid-1800s, the earlier name came back. And unlike many other relic foods of centuries past, they still taste good today, even if you are used to wheat pancakes.

Indian Flapjacks

....

1½ cups cornmeal

½ cup flour

2 eggs, beaten

2 tablespoons sugar, molasses or maple syrup

¾ cup milk

Mix the ingredients and then heat a griddle and spread a little butter or bacon fat on it—or, as Catharine Beecher, sister of Harriet Beecher Stowe and author of Miss Beecher's Domestic Receipt Book, *suggests, "Take a bit of salt pork and rub over with a fork. This prevents adhesion, and yet does not allow the fat to soak into what is to be cooked." Fry "regular round" cakes 3–4 minutes per side until browned. Serve with maple syrup. You can use more or less milk for thinner or thicker cakes.*

Joel Barlow notes that in New England, this common colonial dish "receives a dash of pumpkin in the paste, / to give it sweetness and improve the taste." That is certainly true.

Corn continues to symbolize the collective interaction and influence of Native Americans on the lives of early pioneers, transforming English food habits into American cuisine. We may have other recipes for corn these days, but we should not forget these early treats, especially the joys of traditional Indian pudding. As Barlow tells us near the end of his epic ode:

Delicious grain! whatever form it take,
To roast or boil, to smother or to bake,
In every dish 'tis welcome still to me,
But most, my Hasty Pudding, most in thee.

2

A Carnival of Vegetables

In 1819, Litchfield's famous preacher Lyman Beecher reported that his garden in Litchfield included corn, cabbage, pumpkins, beets, peas, cucumbers, potatoes, pole beans, lettuce, radishes, turnips and carrots, as well as fruit like cantaloupes and raspberries. A few decades later, his daughter and international celebrity Harriet Beecher Stowe lauded the vegetables of her time:

> *Now I sat down all at once to a carnival of vegetables, ripe, juicy tomatoes, raw or cooked; cucumbers in brittle slices; rich, yellow sweet potatoes; broad Lima-beans, and beans of other and various names; tempting ears of Indian corn steaming in enormous piles, and great smoking tureens of the savory succotash, an Indian gift to the table for which civilization need not blush; sliced egg-plant in delicate fritters; and marrow squashes, of creamy pulp and sweetness: a rich variety, embarrassing to the appetite, and perplexing to the choice.*

This wonderful diversity was not anomalous; it was a healthy diet for a nineteenth-century family.

Although corn was king, other vegetables were just as vital. Various woodland plants, such as fiddleheads, were native delicacies and especially important in the early years. Available only a few weeks in the spring, the young ostrich ferns were enjoyed by those in the know. Plants that we might consider "weeds" today were used as well. Young pokeroot was eaten like asparagus, and its more poisonous mature version became insect repellant. The Indians used poke as a snake-bite cure, as well. But as centuries passed and more "garden" or "farm" varieties of vegetables became available, knowledge of these herbs and weeds was slowly lost.

Most people pickled vegetables for the long winters. Mushrooms were pickled with a blade of mace and melted mutton fat. However, most vegetables were preserved in brine or in cider

Beets were one of the few crops transplanted from Europe that became staples in Connecticut. *Courtesy of the Hamden Historical Society.*

vinegar if it was readily available. Amelia Simmons tells us to gather fresh, small cucumbers and "make a pickle of salt and water, strong enough to bear an egg." Boil the brine, pour onto the cucumbers and wait for twenty-four hours. After straining and drying, take fine white vinegar, cloves, diced mace, nutmeg, white peppercorns, long pepper and "races of ginger (as much as you please)," boil all and "clap the cucumbers in" with a few vine leaves and a bit of salt. "As soon as they turn their colour, put them into jars, stive them down close, and when cold, tie on a bladder and leather."

Beans had been combined with corn for succotash by the native tribes and continued to be used in this way by the colonists, mostly in August and September, when both corn and beans were plentiful. The many varieties of beans included clabboard, Windsor, crambury, frost, six week and lazy. The "string beans" among them were eaten fresh, often with an herb sauce made of mint, parsley or rosemary, along with oil, garlic, vinegar, salt, pepper and perhaps cloves.

But of course, common dry beans were used most often by Connecticut households, and always in the fabled iron bean pot. It dangled in the huge fireplace from iron bars or green wood, bubbling for hours, thickened with added cornmeal and seasoned with salt pork. The pot was moved up or down to control the temperature and in and out with iron hooks or forks. Impoverished families may have only used one kettle, spoon and pot, and from this forced ingenuity sprang many of the dishes that became New England staples, including the variations on baked beans.

This is a patient cook's dish, and many did not wait properly, leading to its bad reputation in later centuries. As Lydia Child points out, "Baked beans are a very simple dish, yet few cook them well." She says to put a pound of dried beans in cold water and hang them over the fire overnight. In the morning, rinse a few times in a colander, put in a kettle with a pound of pork, cover with water and "keep scalding hot" for at least an hour. Equal pieces of fat and lean pork are desirable, though the cheeks are the best. Sprinkle pepper on the beans, as this will "render them less unhealthy." She does not mention adding molasses for the "brown" beans we are used to today. However, the following recipe does. You can substitute salt pork in this recipe if you like and use great northern beans or navy beans.

Connecticut Baked Beans

....

2 ½ cups dried beans, soaked overnight

1 pound diced smoked pork jowl

1 medium onion

½ cup maple syrup

½—¾ cup molasses

¼—½ teaspoon ginger

¼—½ teaspoon cinnamon

⅛ teaspoon nutmeg

1 teaspoon Worcestershire sauce

1 teaspoon chopped garlic

6 tablespoons tomato paste dissolved in 1 cup water

After soaking, simmer beans for 2—3 hours on the stove. Drain beans and reserve liquid. Place beans and remaining ingredients, except tomato paste and water, into an oven-safe cook pot with enough reserved liquid to cover the mixture. Bake at 250 for 6—8 hours. With about an hour to go, add tomato paste and water and continue to bake uncovered. A crockpot is useful, and since stoves and ovens vary, not to mention the beans themselves, experimentation may be necessary to get it just right.

When beef became more popular, it was incorporated, as were other available vegetables, leading to dishes like "Monday's Bean Pot" from the *New England Heritage Cookbook*, which includes two tablespoons bacon fat, one pound top round beef, two onions, three carrots, one turnip, two celery ribs, one-fourth cup old-fashioned oats and three potatoes. However, it includes no beans. The "bean pot" was now only a method, and the difficulty of turning dry beans into appetizing meals was a thing of the past.

Squash was the third of the "three sisters" grown by Native Americans and often added to succotash. A variety of squash, including pumpkins, grew in early Connecticut gardens or fields. These and other vegetables provided sustenance but also, more importantly, opportunities for cooks to add color and texture to the table. The large native pumpkins grew "from forty to sixty pounds" and were a much-derided foodstuff, used primarily for making beer or as an additive for bread or pudding rather than food by itself. Pumpkin bread was made with half dried pumpkin and half cornmeal and had an unpleasant appearance. A pumpkin could be stewed whole in its shell, but even then it was looked down on as emergency food. Its seeds were baked, as we eat them today, or boiled into a medicinal jelly. More common was dried pumpkin, an Indian method that provided vegetable fare on a long journey.

Pumpkin pie was not popular until some of the famous "Blue Laws" banned minced pies. Only then did it become a Thanksgiving tradition, replacing the English pies that preceded it. When Lydia Child wrote recipes in the early 1800s, pumpkin pies were still suspect. However, her simple yet tasty recipe no doubt helped make them beloved:

Pumpkin Pie

3 eggs

1 quart milk

Stewed pumpkin

Sweetening—molasses or sugar

2 teaspoons salt

2 teaspoons sifted cinnamon

Lemon rind, grated

The sweetest part is closest to the rind, so stew the pumpkin first, then strain, seed and pare it. Combine eggs, milk and pumpkin and sweeten to taste with molasses or sugar, stirring until thick. Add spices. To make a richer pie, use more eggs; some use a gill (½ cup) of milk. Spoon into a pastry shell and bake 40–50 minutes until done.

Of course, pumpkin was not the only squash variety. Acorn squashes were often pureed and baked, mixed with cream, butter and maple syrup. Sometimes cinnamon or nutmeg was added. A winter squash might be cubed, mixed with brown sugar and butter and baked. If prepared at the right time of year, these dishes could be sublime. Squash soup was much more popular than pumpkin soup, which never caught on in Connecticut. In this recipe, butternut squash is recommended, but others may be substituted:

Squash Soup

....

1 medium or 2 small squash

1 green apple, peeled, cored, diced

1 small onion, diced

3 cups stock

1 tablespoon butter

1 tablespoon flour

1½ cups milk

2 tablespoons brown sugar

Salt and pepper, nutmeg

Peel and chop the squash, removing and saving the seeds. Put the squash, apple and onion in a large sauce pan with stock. Bring to a boil and then reduce to a simmer and cook until soft. Strain vegetables and place in a food processor, reserving liquid. Puree mixture with enough liquid to make it smooth. In the pan, combine butter and flour and cook slightly. Slowly add milk, brown sugar, squash puree and remaining liquid. Bring to a boil, then reduce and cook until the soup becomes thick and creamy. Serve with a sprinkle of nutmeg, a dollop of sour cream and a few roasted squash seeds. These can be made by washing off pulp, salting and spreading on a cookie sheet. Cook at 300 degrees until roasted and crisp, about 25–30 minutes.

Settlers also planted European vegetables like peas, parsnips, turnips and carrots, all of which grew nicely in Connecticut. "Peas" are a plant from Europe, though the Indians grew a small bean that was called a "pea" by the colonists. Peas came in as many varieties as beans, with names like the Crown Imperial, the Rondeheval, Early Carlton, Marrow Fats, Spanish Manrattos and the popular sugar pea. They would be picked carefully from the vines "as soon as the dew is off" and cleaned and boiled immediately for the richest flavor. In spring, a fresh pea soup was made with cream, chicken stock, tarragon, mint and sparkling wine or cider.

Dried peas would be soaked overnight, with a quart of water for every quart of peas. Catharine Beecher says to boil peas in water for sixty minutes, adding a teaspoon of saleratus ten minutes before the end. Change the water and add a pound of salt pork, then boil the soup three to four hours until the peas are soft. If using green peas, then they don't need to be soaked and shouldn't be boiled for more than an hour. When ready to serve, add butter. You could also use a mutton bone, ham bone or roast beef in pea soup, as well as celery and onions.

Turnip soup was also popular, cooked with a crust of bread, white pepper, cloves, onion, mace, nutmeg and herbs. However, New World potatoes were rare in Connecticut during colonial times. One reason was the belief that horses or cows that ate them would die. Those who did use them mixed yellow potatoes with butter, sugar and grape juice from local wild grapes. White potatoes were introduced from Ireland in about 1720 but did not become popular until the 1800s, when Harriet Beecher Stowe points out that potatoes had became a "stanch old friend," like bread, necessary to the table. Roasting and boiling were easy, common methods of preparation, although fried potatoes began to be popular at this time in large, French-inspired restaurants, if not in Connecticut homes. And of course, potatoes became an ingredient in many chowders.

Certain areas in the state grew famous for certain vegetables. Wethersfield had "vast fields uniformly covered with onions," which were exported to places like New Hampshire and Pennsylvania in the late 1700s. People began trading them for items like nutmeg and molasses. However, by 1823, too much competition forced them to focus on seeds, an industry that continues today.

As each generation of immigrants came across the Atlantic, they brought new vegetables. One of the more interesting was lovage, from the eastern Mediterranean, similar to celery, with "large light-green leaves and yellowish flower-umbels" and a strong flavor, sometimes called "smellage." A friend of Mark Twain, Julia Hill Sanford, suggested a recipe for lovage soup made with veal shank, tomatoes, carrots, onions, potatoes and six stalks of the herb.

New generations also brought in new recipes. The following Caribbean *mais Moulin avec pois* parallels the traditional succotash elements. It comes from Selma Miriam and Noel Furie at the classic vegetarian restaurant Bloodroot in Bridgeport. Selma says to use Haitian cornmeal and that "the best chili for this is the 'Jamaican hot pepper.'" It is similar to a habanero but is spicier with "a better scent," giving this dish a spicy kick.

First appearing in Connecticut in the 1720s, potatoes had outstripped corn as a staple crop by the twentieth century, enough to be made into "chips." *Courtesy of the Hamden Historical Society.*

Spicy Haitian Polenta

1½ cups dried kidney beans

3 whole Jamaican hot peppers, seeds and pulp, remove stems

1 green pepper (remove seeds)

2–3 tablespoons fresh thyme leaves

½ cup straight-leaf parsley leaves

2 scallions, cut up

1 medium onion, diced

6 cloves garlic

½ teaspoon ground cloves

2 tablespoons olive oil

3 tablespoons coconut oil

3 cups coarse cornmeal

1 tablespoon salt

3 cups water

Pick over and soak beans overnight or for several hours. Drain and cook in fresh water until very tender. Reserve water. Prepare herb-spice seasoning by placing peppers, thyme, parsley leaves, scallions, onion, garlic and cloves in a food processor. Pulse for 5 minutes until liquefied. Take half the spice mixture and refrigerate or freeze the rest for later use. Sauté the spice mixture in the oils over low heat, stirring often for 10–15 minutes, until it begins to turn golden brown. Add 3 cups of cooked red beans. Continue cooking, tossing the beans with the spice mix for another 5–8 minutes. Meanwhile, measure cornmeal into a bowl. Cover with cold water and swish cornmeal around. Pour off cloudy water, add fresh water and repeat the process. Add three cups of the bean cooking water to the herb and bean mixture. Stir well. Bring to a boil and add salt. Pour off excess water from the cornmeal bowl and add meal to the pot by the spoonful with 3 cups more water. Stir constantly as the mixture is brought to a boil, then cover. Stir well and cook for 15 minutes, adjusting heat as necessary and adding water when polenta gets too thick. Reduce heat and cook for 10 minutes more. Adjust salt and water if necessary to balance the peppers. The resulting "polenta" should have a porridge-like consistency. Serve with slices of avocado, ripe fried plantain or creamed collard greens. The recipe makes a lot but is easily halved.

The Bloodroot polenta, herb colored from the spices, is smooth and creamy and completely vegan. This dish and the others were considered meals in themselves. Our forebears understood the simple truth that even when meat is widely available, vegetables form the basis of a diet, not an afterthought. That is good advice today in an overpopulated world searching for more food.

3

As American As...

In Mark Twain's *A Tramp Abroad*, he gives a comical recipe for New English Pie:

> *To make this excellent breakfast dish, proceed as follows: Take a sufficiency of water and a sufficiency of flour, and construct a bullet-proof dough. Work this into the form of a disk, with the edges turned up some three-fourths of an inch. Toughen and kiln-dry in a couple days in a mild but unvarying temperature. Construct a cover for this redoubt in the same way and of the same material. Fill with stewed dried apples; aggravate with cloves, lemon-peel, and slabs of citron; add two portions of New Orleans sugars, then solder on the lid and set in a safe place till it petrifies. Serve cold at breakfast and invite your enemy.*

Hartford's most famous traveler was making fun of the pie-making foibles of the time more than the celebrated apple. If any food could be considered pure New England, it was this versatile fruit. Wild apples did exist in the New World, though no one is sure how much Native Americans used these sour-tasting specimens. Apple seeds were brought from Europe in the holds of ships and planted immediately after ground was cleared for houses and farms.

By the middle of the 1600s, the trees that colonists planted had grown enough to begin producing a dependable crop. In 1649, Henry Wolcott of Windsor already had a large orchard with several different apple varieties. A few years later, as supplies increased, export became profitable. By the 1700s, Europeans acknowledged that American apples were superior and the climate of Connecticut perfect for the cultivation of these trees.

This versatile fruit was eaten in dozens of ways. Roasted or baked apples were covered with sugar and cream. Slices of fruit were often dried in the autumn and then later soaked in cold water and stewed to reconstitute them. Apple butter came about by taking "new sweet" apple cider, reducing it by half and then boiling it until dark with stewed apples and quinces at a ratio of four to one. This would keep in jars for up to a year. Applesauce was prepared by stewing apples with quince and molasses, cooled and set down in barrels for winter storage. Apple jelly was made by boiling sliced apples without peeling or coring them; mashing and then straining the mixture; beating in egg whites, brown sugar and lemon juice; boiling three times; and leaving the mixture to cool. As Catharine Beecher notes, this could be boiled further to "make elegant apple candy."

We now distinguish between apple dumpling and apple pie, apple pudding and apple custard, but the spectrum at the time had few names, and often those names were applied to different dishes. The recipes only began to be defined when written into cookbooks in the nineteenth century. The names then were retrospective and contradictory, depending on authorship. Though a culinary historian or chef might today create clear distinctions, none has truly existed.

Custard and pudding recipes that included apples were especially diverse, and the two words were used inconsistently and sometimes interchangeably. Both pudding and custard could refer to a boiled mush made from apples, sugar and spice. A "pudding" could be apples baked in a tin dish and served with "thin custard." Or the peeled and cored apples could be put in a tin filled with orange or lemon peel, sugar and cinnamon and baked or simmered until soft. Custard could be poured over this, or the original mixture could have sugar and egg whites mixed with it to make "custard," or "pudding" or a name created by the individual cook that had nothing to do with either.

A "bread pudding" might be made by grating peeled apples into a dish and covering with grated stale bread, then beating in two eggs, a pint of milk, rosewater and grated lemon or orange and baking. Hilda Hanson of Stratford made "apple pudding" by pouring a mix of egg, sugar, butter, flour and vanilla over apples in a pan, switching the crust and filling of a traditional pie. Catharine Beecher's "Birth-day Pudding" was more like bread layered with apples, baked in a pan. "Bird's nest puddings" were another variation and also varied in composition from chef to chef. Catharine Beecher made them by peeling and coring apples without cutting them. These were put whole in a deep dish, sprinkled with mace and filled with a spoonful of sugar. Water was put in the pan surrounding these hollow apples, and the dish was simmered. When the apples were soft, she poured in just enough custard to cover them and baked it.

Apple "crumbs" and "bettys" were just as puzzling. Apple crumb most likely derived from the British recipe called "crumble" and featured a combination of sliced apples topped with a mixture of butter, flour and sugar. Bettys, on the other hand, used bread crumbs instead of flour. Dried currants or cinnamon could be added to both, and whipped cream or ice cream might be scooped on top. You didn't have to use apples for these, either, and rhubarb, blueberries or peaches worked just as well. Just as "crumble" morphed into "crumb," continued tinkering led to "apple crisp," which often includes rolled oats. "Cobblers," too, are found in the lingo, incorporating a biscuit-like topping spooned over the fruit. However, these definitions were malleable and often depended entirely on the cook and, to some extent, the place where they were made. Other names for the same or similar recipes included "apple slump," "apple mose," "apple crowdy" and more.

This orchard owned by John Hale of Glastonbury was one of hundreds that covered the state until blight destroyed them in the early twentieth century. *From Connecticut Circle.*

Of course, the most enduring of the Connecticut apple dishes was pie. Pies had been made with just about any filling for centuries, but something—perhaps the quality of the American apples—made "apple pie" a reborn classic. Author of the *Early American Cookbook* Hyla O'Connor tells us that "early pie crusts were made with meat drippings or lard and would perhaps be tough by today's standards. But the settlers loved pies and sometimes ate them for breakfast. In those days, pies were not made one or two at a time; as many as fifty might be made in the winter, when the baked pies could be frozen. When a pie was wanted, it was brought indoors and set in front of the fire to thaw and warm."

Everyone has a favorite recipe for apple pie, and many have not changed for generations. Amelia Simmons suggested, "Stew and strain the apples, to every three pints, grate the peal [*sic*] of a fresh lemon, add cinnamon, mace, rosewater and sugar to your taste; and bake in paste No. 3." Catharine Beecher's version instructs you to pare, core and cut apples, then line dishes with pastry and insert apples, covering with dough and baking until fruit is tender. Then "take them from the oven, remove the upper crust, and put in sugar and nutmeg, cinnamon or rose water to your taste; a bit of sweet butter improves them. Also putting in a little orange peel before they are baked makes them a pleasant variety." She reminds us that "all apple pies are much nicer if the apple is grated and then seasoned."

Stewing the ingredients first was one traditional way to make pies. However, fresh fruit worked equally well, placed into the pie shell without precooking. Another interesting habit was cooking the pie and opening the top crust in order to season. It's unclear how this was managed, as removing a half-baked pastry from the top of a hot pie seems a difficult and unnecessary step, perhaps explaining why the practice went out of fashion. Many of the old recipes use rosewater, something often left out of modern ones but which should be returned, as both flavor and aroma are enhanced. Mark Twain would probably prefer our modern crusts, however.

Pork Apple Pie, sometimes oddly known as "sea pie," became popular in the state, as well. It contains dried apples, salt pork and molasses. Such a dish was not served as dessert. The pastry was filled with tart, peeled apples and sprinkled with three-fourths cup of maple sugar, a half teaspoon cinnamon and a quarter teaspoon nutmeg, then dotted with twenty pieces of salt pork the size of peas. It was covered with a crust and baked for forty-five minutes in moderate heat.

Sometimes a pie was made without a bottom, but a topless fruit pie was called a tart. They were traditionally made by cooking the fruit first and then placing it on the "paste," or dough. The cooked fruit sets upon cooling. A lattice design of woven pastry strips makes for a nice presentation, but the open apples, perhaps brushed with ginger preserves, shine and glisten. The tart that follows combines an old recipe for "royal paste" and a modern recipe from Hindinger Farm in Hamden:

Spiced Apple Tart

ROYAL PASTE

2 cups flour

2 tablespoon sugar

½ cup butter

2 egg whites

1 egg yolk

Rub flour, sugar and butter together and then blend in egg whites and yolk. Add water, a tablespoon at a time, to form dough. Knead slightly and then chill.

APPLES

½ cup sugar

1 teaspoon cinnamon

5–7 apples

1 teaspoon rosewater

4 tablespoons butter, cut up

½ cup fruit preserves—apricot or ginger

2 tablespoons water

Roll out chilled pastry dough in a tart or pie dish. Preheat oven to 400. Mix sugar and cinnamon. Peel and cut apples into ¼-inch slices. Line the dish with apples in layers and sprinkle each with a little sugar cinnamon mix, overlapping layers until the dish is filled. Sprinkle rosewater on the top and dot with butter. Bake 40 minutes, until browned. Mix preserves and water. Brush mixture onto tart and bake for another 5 minutes until preserves glisten. Serve warm or cooled and dollop with whipped cream.

Throughout the nineteenth century, Connecticut trees continued to supply an abundance of apples. The state grew hundreds of varieties, with examples like Baldwin, Hurlburt, Roxbury Russet and Fallawater being very productive and the Pecks Pleasant and Westfield Seeknofurther being the highest quality. Apple recipes remained popular, as well, and never suffered the backlash that many other colonial standbys did when the region became wealthier. One recipe that became more popular in the 1800s was apple coffeecake, a more "civilized" or "upper-class" dish. Here's a moist, flavorful recipe with great swirls of cinnamon, adapted from *The New England Heritage Cookbook*:

Apple Coffeecake

6 apples

2 cups plus 5 tablespoons sugar

5 teaspoons cinnamon

3 cups flour

3 teaspoons baking powder

1 teaspoon salt

1 cup oil

4 eggs

¼ cup orange juice

1 tablespoon vanilla

Whipped cream

Set oven to 375 degrees. Pare, core and slice apples, then toss the slices with 5 tablespoons sugar and cinnamon and set aside. Sift together flour, baking powder, salt and 2 cups sugar. In a separate bowl, combine oil, eggs, orange juice and vanilla. Pour wet ingredients into dry and mix well. Drain apples of any excess liquid. Grease a Bundt pan or other cake pan and pour in a third of the batter. Spoon half the apple mixture onto the batter. Layer another third of the batter, then remaining apples, and finish with batter. Bake for 75 minutes, until done. Cool before removing from the pan. Serve with whipped cream.

Of course, many scholars maintain that the primary reason people grew apple trees was not for food; rather, it was for cider. Oliver Wolcott's 1649 orchard in Windsor was primarily for "syder," making five hundred hogsheads of it in one year. Apples were harvested when fully ripe, twisted easily from the branch. They were usually "sweated"—stored for several days to improve their sugar content. Then they were ground, separated, pressed and left to ferment, assisted occasionally. Connecticut cider quickly became the most famous in New England, with people like Rhode Island founder Roger Williams praising it effusively. By 1700, so much was being made that it went for only seven shillings a barrel, and every man, woman and child drank it.

Chief Justice Oliver Ellsworth, born in Windsor in 1745, told his son that, when he was a boy, "men in Windsor assembled in each others' houses and would drink out a barrel of cider in one night." This cider was, of course, intoxicating; only in North America, and only very recently, has the word "cider" been used to describe anything but an alcoholic beverage. It was exported to the West Indies and Europe as early as 1741. At the time of the Revolution, one in ten farms

Harvest is a family affair at Holmberg Orchards. Third-generation farmer Richard teaches his son Russell how to select the perfect apple. *Courtesy of Holmberg Orchards.*

included a cider mill, and cider was used for currency, traded for services and other goods. Lyman Beecher's Litchfield family "ate apples" and "drank cider" during the Revolution.

But the best compliment came from the legendary French epicure Jean Anthelme Brillat-Savarin, who dined outside Hartford in October 1794 at the house of a local farmer. He had "a superb piece of corned beef, a stewed goose, and a magnificent leg of mutton, plenty of all sorts of roots, and at each end of the table two enormous jugs of an excellent cider." It was a fresh, sweet cider he could not get in Europe, and he found it "so excellent that I could have gone on drinking for ever."

The New England–style cider historically common in Connecticut was often fortified with molasses or other sweetener and was more concentrated than in some other areas of the country, with a higher alcohol level, natural carbonation and added raisins or currants. Sometimes it was boiled down into sweet cider syrup. This could be used in baking or simply poured hot over a cake or other dish. Hard cider was used as an ingredient for fish, chicken and potato dishes. It was mixed with ice cream and used to preserve other fruits and became a valued addition to any relish. Cider jelly was a staple in kitchens—boiled down slowly, run off onto a sheet and ladled into canning jars. Stratford's Nellie Coe left a recipe from the mid-1800s that soaked four tablespoons gelatin in two cups cold water, while another quart was nearly boiled with two cinnamon sticks. After removing from heat, stir in the gelatin to dissolve and then add a cup of cider, two lemons' worth of juice and three cups of sugar, stirring well. After straining, pour into molds and chill, leaving you with a wonderful jelly.

From 1885 to 1904, San Jose scale (a pest of tree fruit) ruined the apple industry, with 90 percent of the orchards destroyed. Cider ceased to be made and drank, and citizens turned to wine and beer. The remaining apple trees barely survived the harsh winter of 1917–18. But recovery has happened, thanks to replanting, perseverance, know-how and the apple's influence as a useful, delicious and valuable fruit. Apples have experienced a renaissance on menus, as well. Ryan and Kelleanne Jones's amazing restaurant in Tariffville, The Mill at 2T, has taken the old ingredients and flavors of Connecticut food and brought them into the modern age, with delectable dishes like the following new classic:

Slow-Cooked Pork Belly with Apple and Celery Root Soup and Sticky Cranberries

Slow-Cooked Pork Belly

½ cup kosher salt
½ cup granulated sugar
1 teaspoon fennel pollen
4 pounds skinless pork belly
2 cups apple cider reduced by ¾

In small mixing bowl, combine salt, sugar and fennel pollen. Place pork belly on baking sheet with wire rack. Generously coat pork on all sides with cure mixture. Place in 400-degree preheated oven and bake for 1 hour, basting with rendered fat every 10–15 minutes. After 1 hour, turn oven to 300 degrees and continue same process for 2 more hours or until pork is fork tender. Remove from oven and cool overnight. To serve: cut pork into ¾-inch squares and heat slowly in warm oven. When hot, drizzle with apple cider reduction and place on serving platter.

Apple and Celery Root Soup

1 celery root knot	2 parsnips
2 apples	2 cups apple cider
1 small onion	2 cups chicken stock or broth

2 sprigs fresh thyme

2 tablespoons fresh sage chopped

3 strips uncooked bacon

½ clove fresh garlic

1 cup heavy cream

Salt and pepper to taste

Peel and rough chop celery, apples, onions and parsnips. Place in large saucepan, add apple cider and simmer for 5 minutes. Add chicken stock and bring to a simmer. Add fresh herbs, bacon and garlic and simmer for 1 hour or until reduced by a third. Place all ingredients into blender and puree on high for 3—4 minutes (finished when completely smooth). Take soup and strain through fine mesh strainer to take out any existing lumps. Add heavy cream and heat to serve.

STICKY CRANBERRIES

8 ounces water

8 ounces sugar

12 ounces fresh cranberries

In saucepan, combine sugar and water and bring to boil. At boil, add cranberries and reduce to simmer for 10 minutes. When cranberries are soft, remove from the heat and cool. To plate the entire dish, ladle soup into a shallow bowl. The rich, buttery pork belly should be cradled in the thick soup, which complements it perfectly with its sweet, natural taste. Two tablespoons of tangy cranberries on top complete a perfect dish.

While jellies and soups, pies and ciders all point to a vast culinary range, it may be the orchard that captivates us most. The white down of early blossoms invites us into spring, and summer's heat urges the apples to become green or mottled or shapely red. You could do worse than to stroll through a ripe Connecticut orchard on a cool autumn morning, clasp a full apple in your hand and bite into its tart and tasty fruit.

4

Fruits of the Season

One of Noah Webster's proudest accomplishments, other than his dictionary and blue-backed speller, was the peach orchard he kept in the backyard of his New Haven home in the early 1800s. Peaches in Connecticut seem anomalous, but formerly only Georgia surpassed our state in production of this juicy delight. In fact, all kinds of fruit have grown well in the state over the centuries. The Native Americans here gathered strawberries, blueberries, blackberries, elderberries, grapes, currants and whatever else they found to eat fresh or dry. Yankee cooks quickly became skilled with these berries, preserving most of the crop either by drying or storing in bottles.

With bushes, vines and trees populating farms and forests across the state and wild fruit filling baskets and wagons, the bounty needed safeguarding against spoilage, and preserved food was more common than freshly picked. Amelia Simmons tells us that what was not immediately baked into pies would be dropped into a pot and boiled until soft. Afterward, it was strained, and sugar was added, about three cups for every quart of liquor. It was then boiled again. Any reserved fruit was blanched in the liquor and then cooled. Wide-mouthed bottles held the fruit with liquid poured over them. Then the cook would "lay a piece of white paper over them, and cover with oil." Variations were needed for certain fruits; strawberries could be squeezed through a cloth and kept in a stone pot. Apricots, grapes, mulberries, gooseberries, damson plums, cherries, raspberries and currants were preserved in a similar manner, sometimes with added liquor, like apple brandy. Later cooks became more inventive, with recipes like this one for peaches:

Peach Preserves

....

1 large lemon

1 small orange

7 cups ripe peaches

5 cups sugar

½ teaspoon ground ginger or ¼ cup chopped crystallized ginger

½ cup blanched slivered almonds

Combine peeled and chopped lemon, orange and peaches in a stainless steel or enameled kettle and simmer 15 minutes until citrus skins are tender. Add sugar and ginger. Bring to a boil, dissolving sugar. Boil until a candy thermometer registers 220 or until the mixture "sheets off a spoon." Add almonds in the last 5 minutes.

True canning was not practiced in America until the end of the nineteenth century, after W.W. Lyman of Meriden patented airtight fruit jars with a spring-fastened glass top for canning in 1858. The distinctions between jams, preserves and marmalades, in the opposite way of apple dumplings and pies, began to lose clarity at about this time. "Jelly" was always calves' foot jelly and did not become fully associated with fruit until the late nineteenth century, when gelatin became widely available.

Economical cooks used everything they could, including leaves. Lydia Child tells us that the young leaves of the currant bush dried "can hardly be distinguishable from green tea." Catharine Beecher used peach leaves to flavor custard, boiling them in a quart of milk and then mixing this with flour and eggs and using the result for pies or puddings.

Cooks would also make "fruit cheese" to preserve it. You would peel the fruit and clarify half the volume of sugar "by adding water and the beaten white of an egg, stirring and skimming it." Boiling fruit in the syrup all day very slowly, you would mash and stir often, until it became a thick, smooth paste. You would put it in buttered pans to cool and lay them in a dry, cool place. The result could be cut in slices for the tea table.

As eating fresh fruit became a little more acceptable in the

Although wild strawberries found by colonists were plentiful and large, later generations cultivated them on farms. *Courtesy of Hamden Historical Society.*

1700s, preparations that did not call for premade jellies or preserves became more popular as well. Innovations followed and soon included playfully named dishes like grunts and flummeries, both incorporating fresh berries. A grunt used bread crumbs, eggs and sour cream, whipped together and baked for an hour in the oven. A flummery was made as follows:

Raspberry Flummery

4 cups fresh raspberries

1 cup sugar

8 slices white bread, crusts removed

½ cup butter

½ cup cream, whipped

Cook berries with sugar in a saucepan for 10 minutes, uncovered. Stir occasionally. Butter bread and place 4 slices in a 9x9 baking dish, butter side up. Alternate a layer of berries with another layer of bread, finishing with berries. Bake 20 minutes. This could be served chilled, flavored with nutmeg or vanilla and topped with whipped cream.

Throughout the nineteenth century, raspberries and blackberries continued to be staples in every garden, and strawberries remained both garden and farmed fruits. In addition to these native berries, other fruits began to make an appearance in Connecticut. Cherry trees were tried in the late 1700s, with mixed results depending on the microclimate. Mulberry trees were also a huge draw, with the lure of silkworms enticing farmers back to this chancy business time and time again over the centuries. Pears were occasionally grown in the state in the 1800s, but they required constant care and were subject to periodic blights. Some rare pear successes included the Talmadge from Northford and the Woodruff of Guilford.

Cranberries became a much larger crop in the late 1800s, achieving one-fourth of the production of Massachusetts and twice that of Maine. Captain Penfield's eight-acre cranberry meadow in Essex produced an average of nine hundred bushels a year, with a profit of $2,400 a year or more. With precise methods and care, Dennis Tuttle of Madison was able to coax 160 barrels from each acre. All these new fruits needed new preparations, though for convenience many cooks devised all-purpose recipes like this one from Catharine Beecher:

Fruit Fritters

1 tablespoon butter

1 cup milk

1 cup cream

1½ cups flour

1 teaspoon salt

3 eggs

Melt butter into milk and cream. Mix ingredients together and combine with blackberries, raspberries, currants, gooseberries, sliced apples or peaches. Fry in small cakes in sweet lard until golden brown. Eat with a sauce of butter beaten with sugar and flavored with wine, nutmeg or grated lemon peel.

Peaches planted in the 1700s flourished in the early 1800s. The climate seemed perfect, and the 1782 *General History of Connecticut* tells us that "1,000 peaches are produced from one tree." By 1840, peaches were as common as apples, with three million trees in the state. Even small family farms like Clark Hill in Prospect planted peach orchards. Prices were always high, but yields were always uncertain. In a good year, one hundred baskets per acre was a satisfying result. They also required close attention to stave off borer worms. Then, in 1850, many were destroyed by "yellows" disease, causing farmers to replant apples instead. By 1870, there were only a handful of peach orchards left in the state, and they had been joined by plum, nectarine, quince and apricot orchards. Peaches increased again to three million trees by 1911, but ten years later, they had been abandoned again. A few remain, like the largest peach tree in the United States in Madison.

Recipes for peaches included the "pie" standbys, mixed with brown sugar, cornstarch, cinnamon, nutmeg and salt and baked in a sour cream pastry. But with new peach orchards at farms like Holmberg Orchards in Gale's Ferry, new recipes have come onto the scene in the twenty-first century. Here is one from Amy Holmberg's catalogue, combining rich creamy Brie, sweet fresh peaches and a sweet and sour sauce that you will start putting on everything but which goes perfectly with these peachy delights:

Peach and Brie Quesadillas with Lime-Honey Dipping Sauce

SAUCE
2 tablespoons honey
2 tablespoons fresh lime juice
½ teaspoon lime rind, grated

QUESADILLAS
1 cup peaches (about 2 large), peeled and thinly sliced
1 tablespoon fresh chives, chopped
1 teaspoon brown sugar
3 ounces Brie cheese, thinly sliced
4 (8-inch) fat-free flour tortillas
Cooking spray
Chive strips

To prepare the sauce, combine ingredients, stirring with a whisk, and set aside. To prepare quesadillas, combine peaches, chives and sugar, tossing gently to coat. Heat a large nonstick skillet over medium-high heat. Arrange one-fourth of cheese and one-fourth of peach mixture over half of each tortilla and then fold tortillas in half. Coat the pan with cooking spray and cook each quesadilla two minutes on each side or until tortillas are lightly browned and crisp. Remove from pan and keep warm. Repeat this procedure with remaining quesadillas and cut each into three wedges. Serve with sauce and garnish with chive strips, if desired.

Before "pick your own" became a popular recreational event, family members pitched in to gather ripe berries. *Courtesy of Holmberg Orchards.*

Today, Connecticut's "pick-your-own" fruit farms have led the burgeoning local food movement. Places like Lyman Orchards and Jones Family Farms bring in hundreds of people on summer days. New laws have restored farmers' markets to prominence. And the industry is growing in new directions using traditional products. Maple Lane Farms in Preston is the largest producer of black currants in North America and uses them to make a popular, healthy juice called Currant Affair. Grapes are also on the rise due to the booming Connecticut wine industry.

Noah Webster's family in West Hartford grew sweet white grapes in the 1700s, long before his New Haven peach trees became a source of pride. The famous lexicographer may not have recognized some aspects of our landscape today, but he certainly would have recognized this ever-changing landscape of fruit. As he said when describing summer in his 1783 blue-backed speller, which instructed five generations of American children, "They regaled themselves with cherries, strawberries, and other fruits of the season; and they passed the whole day in sporting in the fields." And whether we are playing in the meadows all day or rushing to work, when we bite into sweet, colorful local produce, it's a privilege to be able to enjoy the fruits of home.

PART II

Down the River to the Sea:
Fish and Shellfish

5

More Than Just Chowder

At the turn of the twentieth century, at the dedication of Hubbard Park in Meriden, 250 people gathered for an oyster and clam roast. Mr. Hubbard provided six barrels of clams, roasted over a big fire, on top of the cliff by Castle Craig. He was following a tradition that went back to the coastal Algonquian tribes, who roasted clams at huge celebrations every summer. Puritan settlers found millions of shells heaped in midden piles on Connecticut's beaches, testifying to the longevity of this bivalve's appeal. After a few decades, settlers got over their initial suspicion, and instead of food for the poor, clams became delicacies. They were eaten raw, used in chowder, roasted on barbecue grills and consumed in one hundred other ways by colonial settlers and modern gourmets alike.

Today, you can still get yourself a license and head to the shore at low tide. On the tidal flats, look for the air holes and then dig with your fingers or push the tines of a clam fork into the sand, lift the clam out and put it into a basket. If you are getting clams this way, or even if you're buying them, it's not a bad idea to let them sit for a while in seawater to allow them time to rid themselves of sand. In Connecticut, you will find soft-shell and hard-shell clams. The hard shells are round and, not surprisingly, have a very hard shell. Hard-shell varieties include sea clams, too big to eat raw and usually chopped up to use for clam strips. The hard-shelled quahogs are slightly smaller and used for chowders and stuffings. Cherrystones and littlenecks are both eaten raw or prepared with bacon and bread crumbs as clams casino. Soft-shelled clams are known as steamers and are tasty raw and perfect fried.

If you need raw clams, you could get the fishmonger to shuck them or shuck them yourself. If so, you'll need a large bowl for the juice and a special clam knife, which has a fat, graspable handle and a small, wide blade. As with shucking oysters, a little courage and a bit of practice don't hurt either, since it takes some elbow grease and a steady hand. Use an oven mitt and stick the knife in between the two halves, working it slowly along the top shell, separating the meat and leaving the hinge intact. Pry it open with the knife, carefully catching the juice in the bowl—it's precious. Of course, if you don't need the clams raw, then steaming them open is far easier. A little water in the bottom of a sturdy pan and a few minutes is all it takes for the clams to yawn open. The prized liquor does steam away, but this process is virtually effortless.

Although clams are a versatile food, many associate them with chowder. Certainly, it is a local staple. The Boston and Maine chowders have taken over in the public imagination, probably because the milk makes them easily distinguishable from Manhattan chowder and other concoctions. However, the southern New England version of clam chowder—called Connecticut Clam Chowder in the old books—distinguishes itself through its use of salt pork and water-based broth. You might think this would make it less rich, but you'd be wrong. This potato-thickened broth is actually richer and more flavorful than the "New England" chowder because the clam essence is not diluted with milk.

Though this clear-broth chowder seems to have originated in New London County, it was popular all along the coast of Connecticut. Captain Frank Hancort, who ran the old ferry from Bridgeport to New York, used only the essential ingredients in his version: one quart of clams, steamed open with liquor reserved; a half pound of salt pork; water; sliced onions; and diced potatoes. However, the version below, similar to the one at the Seahorse Tavern in Noank, is probably more appealing to modern tastes with the additional flavoring of leeks and fresh herbs:

Connecticut Clear-Broth Clam Chowder

½–1 cup salt pork, diced

2–3 celery stalks, diced

1 large leek, white and pale green
   parts, diced

1 small onion, diced

3 cups clam juice—from canned
   clams or bottled

2 cups water

2 cups potatoes, diced

1 ½ cups quahog clams, chopped

1 bay leaf

2 teaspoons fresh thyme

Salt

Pepper

2 teaspoons fresh parsley, chopped

Cook salt pork in a large pot over medium heat, rendering fat. Remove cracklings and save. In the drippings, cook diced celery, leek and onion until soft. Add clam juice and water, diced potatoes, clams, bay leaf and fresh thyme. Bring to a boil. Reduce heat and cook until thickened, about 15 minutes. Thicken with slurry of 1 tablespoon cornstarch to 2 tablespoons water if necessary. Season with salt and pepper. Remove from heat and let cool slightly; take out the bay leaf. Serve with cracklings and chopped parsley.

These freshly harvested soft shells at Bud's Fish Market in Branford are ready for steaming and then a little lemon and butter. *Courtesy of the authors.*

Other recipes omit leeks or celery or use Tabasco as flavoring, though all use quahogs, salt pork, potatoes and clam juice as the primary liquid. However, chowder is only a fraction of clam cuisine in Connecticut. During the nineteenth century, many towns built clambake pavilions along the coastline, and hundreds of people attended summer celebrations. Baking the clams in the sand was a time-honored tradition, practiced by local experts, though it led to sandy disaster as often as it led to unbelievable cuisine. After gathering seaweed and cannonball-sized stones, a fire is started in a pit to heat the stones until they are glowing hot. The ashes are swept off to form a bed, and wet seaweed is placed on the stones. The clams and lobsters are arranged on the stones, and wet canvas covers the giant pit, steaming for several hours.

However, if you don't have a beach in your backyard, try this recipe for a different kind of baked clams, adapted from the *Mark Twain Library Cookbook*. You can use canned clams, though for presentation, the shells are needed, so likely you'll use fresh clams and supplement the quantity with canned:

Baked Clams

16 clamshells	¼ teaspoon salt
15 ounces clams, minced or chopped	1½ tablespoons dry sherry
½ cup reserved clam liquor	½ teaspoon Worcestershire sauce
3 tablespoons butter	3 drops Tabasco
3 green onions, finely chopped	1 teaspoon lemon juice
3 tablespoons flour	1 tablespoon chopped parsley
½ cup half and half	Buttered bread crumbs

Drain clams, reserve liquor and set aside. In a medium cooking pan, sauté onions in butter. Add flour and cook slightly. Pour in clam liquor and half and half and cook slowly until thick. Stir in remaining ingredients, except bread crumbs. Add clams and mix. Spoon mixture into clamshells, sprinkle with bread crumbs. Bake at 400 for about 15 minutes.

These methods are only the tip of the clamshell. From complement to featured item, the clam fulfills multiple culinary roles. For example, Catharine Beecher's simple preparation suggests, after opening the clams in "a pot with very little water," to "lay buttered toast in a dish when you take them up" or "put into a batter and fry." Clam pie was popular, with a pastry crust, clams, eggs, butter, cream and pepper. Some even made "clam frappes," a recipe from 1904 that says to wash clams in their shells and place them on the stove in a saucepan until hot, when the juice runs out. Then remove the clams and shells and strain through a fine piece of cheesecloth. Season well with cayenne and paprika and add a very small bit of butter and a little boiling water. When cold, pack in ice for about ten minutes. Serve in small, thin glasses. This fascinating method, related to the oyster cocktail, became a classic amongst Connecticut's elite.

One of the most popular ways was to use eggs and bread crumbs to make small cakes. *The Early American Cookbook* suggests the following recipe, slightly modified:

Clam Cakes

1 quart clams, shucked and minced	1 tablespoon sour cream
½ cup reserved clam liquor	Celery salt
½ cup celery, diced	Black pepper
1 cup cracker crumbs or bread crumbs	Fat or oil for frying
1 egg, beaten	

Drain clams and reserve liquor. If using fresh clams, chop roughly. Combine clams, liquor, celery and bread crumbs, allowing the crumbs to absorb the liquid. Stir in beaten egg and then add sour cream, celery salt and black pepper. If the mixture looks too wet, add more bread crumbs; too dry, some more liquor or water. Form

This iconic sign along Route 1 greets visitors to The Place in Madison, known for its roasted barbecue clams, as well as grilled lobster and bluefish. *Courtesy of the authors.*

small cakes and fry until both sides are brown. Drain on paper towels. Serve with tartar sauce or homemade remoulade. To make clam fritters, use flour instead of bread crumbs and drop into hot fat or lard instead of frying. By adding leftover potatoes to the clam cake recipe, a delicious clam hash results, a specialty of many old-time diners and clam shacks along the coastline.

The clam shacks of Connecticut are legendary. Places like Bart's Drive-In, Sea Swirl and Jimmies have been serving delights like whole-belly clam rolls for decades, inheritors of a long tradition of fresh seafood. A fascinating example is The Place in Madison, started by brothers Gary and Vaughn Knowles in the early 1970s as an open-sky, picnic-style eatery. The chefs use only hickory and oak wood to fire a long, thirty-five-foot grill, and the smokiness embeds in all the items, whether grilled, roasted or steamed in trembling pots. The chefs wear rubber boots, and visitors sit on tree-stump seats under the sun or a red-and-white tent, depending on the weather. Most places that call themselves "clam shacks" wish they had this kind of authenticity.

One of their specialties is roasted barbecue clams. The method is classic; as Catharine Beecher tells us in her 1846 cookbook, "Thin-edged clams are the best ones. Roast them in a pan over a hot fire or in a hot oven, placing them so as to save the juice. When they open, empty the juice into a sauce-pan, and add the clams with butter, pepper, and very little salt." The open-flame barbecue is more modern, and strangely rare, since the results are absolutely delicious.

Roast Barbecue Clams

1 dozen littleneck clams
¼ cup barbecue sauce
½ stick butter
Lemon wedges

Prepare charcoal grill or preheat gas-fired grill. Place clams on the grill and cover; cook until the shells open, about 5–10 minutes. Remove the tops and brush the barbecue sauce onto the clam meat, along with a thin pat of butter. Cook an additional 5 minutes until the sauce glazes. Serve with lemon wedges.

Connecticut's shellfish population continues to evolve, and not just because of the influences of new cultures and cuisines. Invasive species have been a problem since Europeans first arrived, but in recent decades, they have become more and more problematic. One such invasive species, Asian shore crabs, began to appear in Long Island Sound in the early 1990s. Their ability to reproduce quickly made them "the most dominant crabs living in the rocky intertidal zone." Varying in size from a pinhead to a quarter, they feed on young clams, depleting our heritage.

Innovator Bun Lai, chef at Miya's Sushi in New Haven, has a solution elegant and economical enough for Lydia Child herself. "Rather than using the most popular types of seafood for sushi, which are often caught or farmed in a way that is ecologically destructive, at Miya's we chose to focus on invasive species because many of them are abundant and destructive of habitats." He harvests a number of invasive species, including Asian shore crabs, and serves them up for a tasty meal. These crabs are clean enough to be harvested anywhere that the water is certified for shellfish. If you decide to gather them yourselves, or if more fish markets begin to carry them, Bun suggests the following preparation:

Asian Shore Crab (Kanibaba)

12–25 shore crabs, depending on size
Olive oil
Lime juice
Sea salt
1 bag non-GMO popcorn

Rinse the shore crabs in cold water. Put the batch in a strainer and then drop them into a pot of rapidly boiling water. The crabs are fully cooked when they turn bright orange. Strain and let them dry in the strainer. Heat olive oil to 350 degrees. Test the oil with one crab; if the crab starts bubbling a lot, the oil is ready for the rest. Don't crowd the oil with too many crabs; this cools the oil and oversaturates it with water. Let the crabs fry until no more bubbles appear. Take the crabs out and let drain on old newspaper. Transfer the crabs to a bowl, squeeze lime juice over them and then sprinkle on sea salt and any spices that tickle your fancy. Mix all the ingredients together and then toss the crabs in a big bowl of freshly popped popcorn.

Bun Lai's pioneering combination of environmentalism and cookery will hopefully spread and ensure, among other things, that Connecticut's beloved bivalves remain in chowders and on half shells for centuries to come, bringing an ocean of history to our mouths and stomachs.

6

Our Own Particular Fish

While visiting Connecticut two hundred years ago, French diplomat Talleyrand's daily food consisted of "smoked fish, ham, potatoes, beer, and brandy." What kind of smoked fish? We're not sure, and since over two hundred kinds of fish were caught here, it could have been anything from striped bass or flounder to pike or perch. Most likely, the menu featured the leaping trout of the rivers and lakes, the seasonal shad or the Sound's roving bluefish.

Long before Talleyrand arrived, the Pequots of southeast Connecticut depended on the bounty of the rivers, streams and ocean for their protein. The Paugusetts built sophisticated weirs on the Housatonic River to catch shad and bass. As Mr. Higginson noted in 1630, "Though New England has no tallow to make candles of, yet by abundance of fish thereof it can afford oil for lamps." Fish was always eaten on Saturday evenings by colonials, usually a "dun-fish."

In the early 1700s, local families used salt from Spain and Portugal to preserve salmon for home use because it was so little liked that no one could sell it. Soon, salmon were fished out, to be replaced with their tender cousin, the trout, which Reverend Lyman Beecher caught by the millpond in Litchfield in his youth. Some Connecticut fishermen went out into the Atlantic to fish for the wonderful cod, to be salted and sold on the European markets. However, it was considered a Massachusetts fish, though many here certainly ate it.

By the nineteenth century, people ate more fresh and less salted fish. Many were fried, especially tasty boneless fillets of salmon or trout. Lydia Child urges cooks to make sure the fat is boiling hot, saying, "It is very necessary to observe this." She suggests dipping fish in cornmeal before frying and using salt pork drippings rather than just lard. To keep the fish fresh and sweet, clean it, wash it, wipe it, sprinkle salt inside and out and keep it on the cellar floor until ready to cook. If you live "far from a seaport," wet the fish with a beaten egg before dipping it in the Indian meal.

To accompany trout or other fish, a gravy was made by taking the leftover frying fat and adding a little butter, flour, boiling water and perhaps vinegar. Lucy Emerson recommends to "fry some parsley green and crisp, melt anchovy and butter, with a spoonful of white wine" to go with trout. Catharine Beecher gives a recipe for "Burnt Butter," which tells us to "heat two ounces of butter in a frying pan, till dark and brown, then add a tablespoonful of vinegar, half a teaspoonful of salt and half a dozen shakes from the pepper box." In recent years, trout have taken the place of salmon as the prime river catch for the table, though the more adventurous chefs and eaters also continue to work with rarer local fish like pike and perch. The following recipe incorporates Beecher's butter sauce nicely:

Sweet Potato Trout

2 sweet potatoes
6 ounces butter, divided
Nutmeg and pepper
2 trout fillets
2 tablespoons balsamic vinegar

Peel and chop sweet potatoes, boil until soft and mash with 2 ounces butter. Season with pepper and nutmeg. Broil fillets 5–6 minutes on high and plate over mashed sweet potatoes. Heat 4 ounces butter until it browns, stirring frequently. Remove from the heat before stirring in balsamic vinegar, so it will not splatter when added. Spoon burnt butter sauce over both and serve.

Of course, Long Island Sound has always been the prime focus of Connecticut's fishing culture. Striped bass has been a sport fish here since the middle of the nineteenth century. Rarer is the black sea bass, a white fish with a dark black skin, better for eating but not as good for sport. But Connecticut's "own particular fish" is the bluefish. It is a recreation fish like the striper, but commercial fishermen also harvest it. Bluefish is notoriously cannibalistic and feeds in much the same way as shark, herding smaller fish and feasting.

Sporting enthusiasts love the bluefish because it fights with the power of a fish many times its size. But diners love the bluefish for its distinctive, if slightly oily, taste. Many eat bluefish simply, but barbecuing works, as does smoking. Smoked bluefish loses its oily flavor and tastes like smoked trout. In *Lymes' Heritage Cookbook*, Arthur Howe tells us that there is no better preparation than smoking it and making pâté.

To make pâté, use an eight-pound (or larger) bluefish. Fillet upon catching, right on the water, and cut smaller depending on size. Put the fillets layered in salt in a nonmetallic container for ninety minutes. Wash and dry the fish thoroughly. Put your smoker outside, protected from the elements. Start up the cooker, using commercial woodchips if you want, or cut your own from hickory or apple trees. Put two pieces of fish on each level of the smoker racks. Close tightly and add more wood every few hours. Smoke for eight hours and then check your progress,

Fishing guide Terry Rand holds up a freshly caught bluefish at the mouth of the Connecticut River. *Courtesy of David Lehman.*

continuing if needed. Test for saltiness and dryness. When you are ready to serve, put fish, onions and mayonnaise in the food processor and mix. Pack the pâté and freeze any that won't be used right away. He reports, "Gorgeous dames continue to throw themselves at my feet proclaiming they would do anything for more of that marvelous smoked bluefish."

Not only will bluefish smoke nicely, but also many people swear that bluefish salad beats tuna salad any day. Take leftover bluefish and flake white meat into a mixing bowl; add chopped onions, salt, pepper, fresh or dried dill weed and mayonnaise, and you have yourself a bluefish salad that goes well on a sandwich, especially a "melt." Pickling bluefish like herring is also delicious. Take skinned fillets and slices of onion and layer in a large casserole. Boil white and red vinegars, salt, sugar and pickling spice, then cool and pour the mixture over the fish and onions. This keeps in the fridge for up to a month.

In the nineteenth century, a popular preparation was baked bluefish covered with slices of salt pork and milk in a dish. It is also good just roasted in aluminum foil on a grill with lemon and butter. Like any good fish, it can be eaten as a sandwich, a salad, in crepes, in a cocktail like shrimp, in stew or in chowder. You can bake it with cream, honey and cornmeal or peanuts. You can eat it stuffed with shallots and pine nuts or mixed with potatoes as hash. You can poach it, sauté it with bacon and onion or make fritters. Here's a recipe for baking it whole:

Baked Whole Bluefish

1 bluefish	2 lemons
½ cup olive oil	½ cup white wine
Fresh herbs	¼ cup water
1 large red onion	1 cup small mushrooms
½ cup butter	¼ pound cherry tomatoes, halved

Grease a shallow baking pan with olive oil and then put the fish into the pan. Fish should be gutted and cleaned, leaving the head on and the belly sliced to stuff. Fill belly with herbs and onion. Drizzle more oil onto the fish and sprinkle with additional herbs, pepper and salt. Put small slices of butter and slices of lemon on top and then fill pan with wine and water. Cook one hour at 250. Add mushrooms and tomatoes and bake for an additional 10–15 minutes. Let stand in the pan for 15 minutes and then remove the fish and serve. Garnish with fresh herbs, tomatoes and lemon wedges.

Although the bluefish looms large, the state fish of Connecticut is the shad, a large member of the herring family, whose Latin name is *Alosa sapidissima*, meaning "most delicious." For Native Americans, the shad's spring arrival was a seasonal blessing, and the tribes would gather on the banks of the Quinnehtukqut to harvest and feast every spring. Salt shad from the Connecticut River fed the Continental army during the Revolutionary War. And Mark Twain mentioned "Connecticut shad" as one of the dishes he was craving while traveling the world in *A Tramp Abroad*.

Connecticut fishermen salted the plentiful shad, packed them in barrels and exported them to the rest of the eastern seaboard. For some reason, even though they were a delicacy elsewhere, shad only had a cult following here. Like its Connecticut friend the bluefish, shad is oily, with a distinctive taste. Unlike easy whitefish that taste like nothing, shad is an acquired taste, and therefore some did not want to bother. Besides, they were so plentiful that some farmers used them as fertilizer or fed them to pigs. Of course, so was salmon, and it wasn't until the 1800s that either of these fish became popular among any but the poorest households. Amelia Simmons says in the 1796 *American Cookery*:

I have tasted Shad thirty or forty miles from the place where caught and really convinced that they had a richness of flavor, which did not appertain to those taken fresh and cooked immediately, and have proved both at the same table, and the truth may rest here, that a Shad 36 or 48 hours out of water, may not cook so hard and solid, and be esteemed so elegant, yet give a higher relished flavor to the taste.

By 1880, the *Sportsmen's Gazetteer and General Guide* showed shad fishing was popular in both the Housatonic and Connecticut Rivers. One reason for this is they hit any lure, even though they are not feeding but exist on their own fat while going upstream, as salmon do. And they fight, twisting, turning and jumping. You can spend an hour or two reeling in a fairly average five-pound shad. The largest caught in the Connecticut River was eleven pounds, four ounces—quite a big fish.

During the 1800s and early 1900s, fishing piers on the river had small shacks on them, which served two purposes: men could sleep there between shad runs, and the fish could be salted. The fish fries that attended these shad runs were for men only and included liberal quantities of rum punch, as well as wrestling and feats of strength. Huge cooking fires on the banks were surrounded by "planked shad." Planking involves nailing fillets and bacon onto an oak board with large-head nails, two in the top and two in the bottom. Put the board eighteen inches from a roaring fire at a sixty-degree angle away from the flames for about forty minutes and flip halfway through. Wearing heavy mitts, remove the nails from the plank and plate the fish.

This method also avoids the main problem with shad: their 1,300 bones, which often refuse to conform to a precise pattern. Also, the meat is pale and delicate and can be overcooked easily. Still, most people admit that the meat is one of the (possibly *the*) best whitefish you can eat, but they don't bother due to the surfeit of bones. You can pick up the meat with a fork (or your fingers, as some swear by) to see and feel the bones. Regardless, boning a fillet is not easy, so get one prepared by an expert if you can.

If you have fillets, you can eat them baked in parchment with garlic, shallots, white wine, lemon and dill. You can bake it in cream and herbs. Or you can stuff the fish with turkey stuffing, baking it for thirty-five minutes at 350 degrees, and eat it that way, picking through the bones and scales. The meat tastes a little nutty, and something like turkey stuffing enhances that flavor. Or perhaps it is the other way around.

One book suggests filling a baking pan with two or three cups of water. Put the shad on a rack in the baking pan to keep it out of the water, adding celery, bay leaf and onion to the water if you have them. Then, bake for five hours with a cover on. You read that right: five hours at 300 degrees. Baste the shad often and pour more water in the dish if necessary. Right before taking the fish from the oven, take off the cover and let it brown. Here's another recipe that takes less time:

The treachery of slippery rocks will not scare off this intrepid fisherman luring trout into the shallower pools.
Courtesy of the Bridgeport History Center.

Baked Connecticut River Shad

....

1 shad, cleaned and split
1½ teaspoons salt
1 teaspoon pepper
¼ cup butter
Parsley, chopped
1–2 lemons

Set oven to preheat at 400. Wash and dry fish. Put into a greased baking dish. Season with salt and pepper and then dot with butter. Bake 25–30 minutes, until done. The fish should flake nicely. Serve with chopped parsley and lemon wedges. Like salmon, shad's fat "self-seasons" the fish when cooking and "bastes" itself.

Some say the best part of the female shad is the roe, which comes in two lobes surrounded by thin membrane. The lobes can be pan fried in bacon fat. They are great with scrambled eggs, especially since they are not as briny or strong as caviar. Some like roe with cucumber salad, first simmering the sac with onion and bay leaf in water for twenty minutes or so. Then, cool and cut the sac into slices, marinating them with French dressing and adding cucumber, mayonnaise and maybe lettuce. However, the most common way to eat shad roe is grilled or broiled with bacon:

Broiled Shad Roe

....

1 pair shad roe
4 slices bacon
2 tablespoons melted butter
Lemon wedges

Preheat the broiler. Make sure to start the roe sacs at room temperature, perhaps in a warm-water bath on the counter. Lay three pieces of bacon perpendicularly on a broiler pan. Place one roe sac close to the edge of bacon and roll slowly and gently until roe is wrapped. Repeat with second sac and then broil 5 minutes per side 4–5 inches from the heat. Broil a minute or two longer on either side, until bacon is crispy. Check the center for doneness; the parts where bacon has wrapped it will cook slower. Drizzle with butter and lemon. The roe may have a bitter aftertaste if not cooked through. Up front you'll taste very mild fish notes, a freshwater taste, not like salmon eggs or caviar.

Some people also like the "milt" of the male shad. The pink lobes look similar to the female's but are much flatter if you look at them side by side. Inside, the milt looks completely different, of course. It is best sautéed in butter and oil after being salted, peppered, floured and spread on toast.

Other fish have recently thrived in Connecticut's waters, from little skate to red hake, and have made their way to our tables. Hopefully, they won't completely replace our traditional fare, and we can balance the old and the new. Whatever the case, the sport of catching our own particular fish will no doubt always serve as prelude to the extraordinary art of cooking them.

7

The Raw and the Fried

In *A Tramp Abroad*, Mark Twain wrote about the horrors of dining in foreign hotels, especially the "sameness" of the bill of fare. He wrote up his own list of dishes he craved, and oysters appeared more often than any other item on the list, with fried and stewed versions second from the top, as well as blue points on the half shell, oyster soup and roasted in the shell "Northern style." He didn't develop his love for these bivalves in landlocked Missouri but rather at his new home in Hartford, probably at the Honiss Oyster House on State Street. By the time Twain moved here, oysters were more than a tradition; they were a beloved delicacy.

In fact, as early as four thousand years ago, people ate oysters in what is now Connecticut. When European colonists arrived in New England, they found the oysters larger and more numerous than those in Europe. The oyster banks seemed like coral reefs, with some specimens achieving a staggering foot in length. At Milford Point, a large heap of shells covered twenty-four acres, the largest Indian "kitchen midden" in New England. Heaps of shells like this were used for paving roads. The species of oysters, called "Eastern," became desirable to everyone, especially the rich foodies of London and Paris in the 1600s. Thus, Connecticut was the first state to grant vested rights in oyster grounds and produced a disproportionately huge percentage of American oysters, shipping them to England, Holland, France and Germany.

Oysters grow in coves, bays and river mouths, and the further protection of Long Island makes the Sound perfect for them to thrive. Connecticut's industry expanded throughout the 1700s, leading to the need for regulation. In 1763, Milford imposed a penalty of one pound on anyone harvesting oysters between April and September, raising it to five pounds a few years later. In 1789, Branford regulated the catching of oysters centered at Stony Creek by the Thimble Islands. However, by the early 1800s, the oyster beds were depleted from overfishing.

Blue points were originally named for a village on the far side of Long Island, but today they are the Sound's most popular oyster. *Courtesy of the authors.*

Then, in 1835, a Fair Haven man named William Townsend imported oysters from down South, beginning a second stage of cultivation and harvesting. In 1849, and again in 1855, the state government regulated oyster farming by declaring that "no one person shall have set out to him territory exceeding two acres." In Greenwich, near the mouth of the Mianus River, extensive naturally occurring beds rarely needed cultivation, but oysters began to be farmed there after 1850. Flat-bottomed oyster boats scoured the Sound throughout the 1800s, using "tongs," a giant pair of scissors attached to a rake, to pull the oysters from their beds. In 1878, Captain Henry Lockwood built a steam-powered oyster boat, the first in the United States.

In 1905, the Standard Oyster Company began operating in several places in Long Island Sound, harvesting large beds near Fairfield and Bridgeport. By this time, all the natural oyster beds were gone, replaced everywhere by aquaculture farming. Unlike fish farms, these oyster farms are simply places for the bivalves to grow naturally and are a huge help to the environment. Oysters filter fifty gallons of water each day, removing nitrogen. Their artificial reefs also provide centers of biodiversity. Without them, not only are we deprived of an excellent food source, but also the environment, the *merroir* they live in, is far poorer for it. Moreover, oysters are good for you: low in saturated fat; a great source of omega-3 fatty acids; and full of iron, copper, iodine, magnesium, calcium, zinc, manganese and phosphorus.

The oysters in the Sound today are often "blue points," named for a small village on the other side of Long Island. Blue points are generally tougher than oysters from, say, the West Coast of America, and the taste is not as pronounced, but it's clean and takes a lot of flavor from the *merroir*. The ones you get today are most likely from the Norwalk area, dredged after spending a few fruitful years growing there. They are extremely mild, perfect for a beginner. When you graduate from those, you might try the rarer Whale Rock oysters from Noank, with wonderful, deep shells and mineral-rich notes.

To taste oysters properly, you must eat them raw. If you've never done it before, this can be a challenge. Plated at the restaurant, they come on the half shell, shucked and ready to go. If you're so inclined, you can shuck them yourself or have your local fishmonger do it for you. Cradle the shell in your hand and examine it. You may notice that it is covered in small, crater-shaped limpets. Despite making the oyster less presentable (though a true oysterphile sees only a thing of beauty), the more of these tiny mollusks on it, the better the oyster probably is. Those little limpets know a good meal when they find one. Hopefully, the oyster meat is not broken, the sign of a poor shucker. Now, forget your teeth and tip the oyster into your mouth, careful not to cut the edges of your lips on the shell. Let it slip whole into your throat and swallow. Blue points tend to be sweet and salty at first, with firm, meaty bodies. The finish is buttery and woody, like an oaked chardonnay. Speaking of which, you could not do better than to wash one down with a local Connecticut white wine.

To improve on a fresh oyster slurped down in its brine is a difficult task. But you don't have to eat raw oysters to eat them in Connecticut style. People stuffed and drenched chicken in them, pounded them into sauces and ate them floured and fried for breakfast. One option popular in Connecticut over the centuries was scalloped oysters. The author of the *Lymes' Heritage Cookbook* notes that growing up in Manchester, she always had this delicious dish at Christmas. As an adult, remembering it fondly, she searched for the recipe for thirty years before finding it:

Old-Fashioned New England Scalloped Oysters

1 pint oysters

6 tablespoons cream

½ cup fine bread crumbs

1 cup cracker crumbs

½ cup plus 3 tablespoons butter

Salt and paprika

Drain oysters, reserve liquid and then add liquid to cream. In a separate bowl, mix bread and cracker crumbs. Grease a baking dish and line it with a third of the crumbs; add oysters in a layer, season and pour half the cream and oyster mixture. Repeat layers—crumbs, oysters, cream—and then pour ½ cup melted butter over the whole dish. Finally top with crumbs and pour the remaining 3 tablespoons of butter over it. Bake at 400 for 20 minutes. Some recipes use scalded milk, while others suggest seasoning the dish with mace. Lydia Child advised skillet heating the oysters in their shells before opening.

Though we might associate oyster sauce with Asian cooking today, our forebears in Connecticut used it constantly, the way we now use ketchup. To make it, Catharine Beecher writes: "Take a pint of oyster juice, add a little salt and pepper, and a stick of mace, boil it five minutes and then add two teaspoonfuls of flour, wet up half a tea-cup of milk. Let this boil two minutes, then put in the oysters and a bit of butter the size of an egg; in two minutes, take them up."

Oyster pancakes were made by mixing a half pint each of oyster juice and milk; adding a pint of wheat flour, a handful of oysters, two eggs and salt; and dropping spoonfuls of the mixture into hot lard. Oyster pie was made by simmering oysters in a frying pan with enough liquor to keep from burning; seasoning with mace, grated nutmeg, whole peppercorns, lemon peel, minced celery and butter; and then baking the results in a pie crust with flour, eggs and occasionally other items like potatoes. This could be served warm or cold.

This natural combination of pastry crust and oysters came to an interesting culmination with "oyster tricorns," a popular party dish in the 1800s:

Oyster Tricorns

8 ounces oysters, well drained
⅛ teaspoon black pepper
¼ teaspoon whole celery salt
1 tablespoon finely chopped sage

1 tablespoon plus 1 cup flour
¼ teaspoon ground nutmeg
½ cup butter
⅛ to ¼ cup water

Chop oysters roughly. In a medium-sized bowl, sprinkle oysters with pepper, celery salt, sage and 1 tablespoon of flour. Toss gently and set aside. Combine the remaining flour and nutmeg. Cut the butter into small pieces and rub it into the flour mixture with a fork or pastry blender. Add the water, a tablespoon at a time, and mix until dough forms. Roll the dough out to ⅛-inch thickness. Cut the dough into 2-inch squares and put a teaspoon of oysters in the center; then fold the corners down to make a triangle. Crimp the edges and place tricorns on a baking sheet. Bake at 425 degrees for 10 to 15 minutes, until lightly browned. Serve as appetizers with a dipping sauce—perhaps one with sour cream, a little lemon juice and chopped capers.

Poulette oysters were another popular appetizer and afternoon snack. According to Louise Bunch in *Connecticut Magazine* in 1900, they consisted of a tablespoon of flour, a lump of butter, a half cup of milk, a pinch of salt and two tablespoons water. Bring it all to a boil in a chafing dish, "stirring constantly." When it is the consistency of heavy cream, pour in a pint of oysters. Cook until the oysters begin to curl at the edges (or "frill," as she calls it), and season with white pepper. The result would be served on toast.

Pickling oysters was a popular way to keep and eat them, until the late twentieth century, when the improved shipping industry made getting fresh oysters easier for inland locales. You would boil them in their own liquor; "take vinegar that is not very sharp" (dilute if necessary); add mace, peppercorns and cloves; and heat until "scalding hot." When vinegar and oysters are lukewarm, you would bottle them. In addition to enjoying the pickled variety, some people created oyster drinks. According to Louise Bunch, one such recipe consisted of a punch glass with six oysters and their liquor, a teaspoon of vinegar, a teaspoon of ketchup, a teaspoon of horseradish, a squeeze of lemon and a drop of Tabasco, served cold.

Oyster soup was popular as well and made a nice alternative to chowder. Catharine Beecher writes: "Put a gallon of water to a knuckle of veal, boil it and reduce to two quarts, strain and add the juice of the oysters you are to use. Add pepper and salt to your taste. Fifteen minutes before taking it up, put in the oysters. Ten minutes before taking it up, put in eight rolled crackers, and after it stops boiling, add half a pint of milk." In *New England Cookery*, Lucy Emerson says to use a fish stock and the yolks of ten hard eggs, along with nutmeg and diced bread. Well-liked versions were similar to the following "stew" from the *Mark Twain Library Cookbook*:

Oyster Stew

....

½ pint fresh oysters

2 tablespoons butter

1 teaspoon salt

Celery salt, a few dashes

1 tablespoon Worcestershire sauce

1 pint half and half

2 cups whole milk

Black pepper

Combine oysters with butter, salts and Worcestershire in a large saucepan and sauté until the oysters begin to curl at the edges. Add cream and milk and heat until mixture just begins to boil. Remove from heat and season with pepper. Serve immediately or cool and reheat.

By far the most popular way to eat oysters, other than raw, was fried. Fried oysters were the favorite food of our sixteenth president, Abraham Lincoln. But like Mark Twain, this Kentucky-born, Illinois-raised lawyer did not eat them as a childhood treat. After his 1860 campaign tour stormed through Connecticut, stopping at Norwich, Hartford, Meriden and New Haven, he found himself in Bridgeport at 10:27 a.m. on March 10, where at the house of Charles Wood on Washington Avenue he first tasted fried oysters. Honest Abe was enchanted. After winning the presidency, he ate these protein-packed treats as often as possible.

Making this dish is simple, using the basic battering and deep-frying method. DeWitt's *Connecticut Cookbook* tells us: "Take those that are large and drain them well, dip them in the beaten yolk of an egg to which a small quantity of cream has been added, roll them in flour, bread or cracker crumbs, and fry quickly in equal proportions of butter and lard." Lucy Emerson recommends frying them in clarified beef suet rather than lard.

— H. J. LEWIS, —

GROWER AND WHOLESALE DEALER IN

SEED, SHELL, AND OPENED

CONNECTICUT NATIVE OYSTERS,

STRATFORD, CONN.

This advertisement testifies to the popularity and plentitude of native oysters in the early part of the twentieth century. *Courtesy of Bridgeport History Center.*

"Finely grated bread crumbs are best, as cracker crumbs become sodden and indigestible." In her classic book, *Consider the Oyster,* American epicure M.F.K. Fisher states that fried oysters "can be one of the best dishes anywhere." However, she points out that many restaurant versions use too much batter and fat, and this is definitely something to avoid when making them at home.

At Match, a restaurant opened by Scott Beck in 1999 in South Norwalk, chef Matt Storch prepares fried oysters in a fascinating way. He layers the fried oyster in a delicious combination he calls a "carpetbagger"—fried oysters topped with steak tartare and truffles. He recommends battering the oysters in half white flour and half semolina. The oysters are then sandwiched in the shell, beginning with a layer of warm truffle cream, the hot fried oyster itself and then cold steak tartare, topped with cold truffle aioli. The components of the dish are as follows:

Carpetbaggers

STEAK TARTARE

1 pound beef top round, fat removed	*1 tablespoon cracked black pepper*
2 shallots	*1 ounce chopped black truffle peelings*
4 tablespoons extra virgin olive oil	*2 teaspoons truffle oil*
2 tablespoons kosher salt, or to taste	*2 tablespoons parsley, chopped*

Place the beef top round in the freezer overnight. The following day, remove the beef top round and defrost for about an hour. Using an automatic slicer or a very sharp knife, slice the beef top round as thin as possible. Take the slices, chop them very fine and place in refrigerator. Peel and dice the shallots. Finally, remove the chopped beef from the refrigerator and mix in the extra virgin olive oil, salt, pepper, truffles, truffle oil, parsley and shallots. Taste for seasoning.

Black Truffle Aioli

2 egg yolks
1 ounce black truffle peelings
1 teaspoon lemon juice
3 tablespoons black truffle oil
2 cups blend oil
Salt and pepper to taste

In a food processor, add egg yolks, truffle peelings and lemon juice. Slowly add truffle oil and blend oil to form an emulsion. Season and chill.

Truffle Cream

2 tablespoons butter
2 shallots
½ cup brandy
4 tablespoons black truffles, finely chopped, with oil
Thyme
1 cup heavy cream

Sweat butter and shallots. Add brandy and flame and then add black truffles and thyme. Add heavy cream and truffle oil and reduce. Finally, after reduced by a quarter, puree in a blender. Feel free to add a few slices of fresh truffle on top of each oyster.

Match's modern twist on traditional fare certainly would have pleased Abraham Lincoln, who served the classic version of his favorite dish on election day in 1864. Mark Twain, too, ever on the hunt for new adaptations of the familiar, would delight with fellow epicures who today enjoy the huge annual oyster festivals in Milford and Norwalk, celebrating and feasting on this iconic delicacy. But even as contemporary tasters enjoy the marriage of old and new and savor both the raw and the fried, oystermen continue to struggle. After disease depopulated the Sound in the late 1990s, it no longer has the crystal-clear water described by the first Europeans. The loss to both the environment and the stomach is a disaster on a statewide, even national, scale. Valuing the many tastes of these little Connecticut miracles is our first step to reversing this tragedy.

8

The Lobster's Finest Role

So you're sitting at a Connecticut seafood shack in front of a freshly steamed lobster. Perhaps you've never done this before, or done it poorly. It's time to stop being intimidated, prepare to get dirty and lose all sense of decorum in your plastic bib. The company you're with and a glass of local white wine or cold beer will move you right along.

Begin with the sweet meat of the claws, which will give you momentum for the more difficult parts. Twist the entire claw until it detaches from the body. Search the nooks of the joints for meat; here, the tines of a small cocktail fork can be useful, though a full-sized fork is too big. Split the large claws with your nutcracker, hammer or mallet to fracture the shell enough to open. Pulling out the small seizer claw first will remove the boney fiber inside the large shell. The trick is to not tear the meat itself. If you're lucky, the claw meat will come out in one piece; look out for loose shell pieces.

To the amateur, the eight small legs seem like a nuisance and worthless to pursue. But good, sweet meat hides there, so pull off one at time and get to it. You can crack the softer parts of the leg shell with your fingers. Some say the best way to access the meat is to suck it out or squeeze it out using your teeth, but a rolling pin also easily removes meat from these small legs.

At a restaurant, the tail may be split for you, but it's easy to gently run your knife down the center of the tail shell's underside. Then remove the tail from the body with a twist. You'll know right away if you've scored a female, since bright red roe will sprinkle out. The tomalley in its signature gray-green color will also emerge once the tail is off. It's easily scraped off or enjoyed as part of the treat. There's more of that in the belly, and many swear that its flavor is the true prize of lobster eating. Others mix it in soup. A boiled lobster will also have quite a bit of water inside, so draining your plate from time to time will be necessary.

Meanwhile, if you're not splitting the tail open and wiggling out the meat, crack the fan end and then push the entire tail through the shell. If you're so inclined, cut into bite-sized pieces or just dip the whole thing into your cradle of melted lemon butter and bite off a little at a time, savoring every morsel of this rich delight. You'll soon be an expert, like world-famous chef and Madison resident Jacques Pepin, who says, "I eat a lot of lobster in the summer, living as I do on the coast of Connecticut. I usually steam it and serve it with corn on the cob and potatoes."

The Fulton Fish & Meat Market

JOHN MOORE, MGR.

Dealers in Fresh and Cured Meats, Fresh and Salt Fish, Oysters, Clams, Scallops and Lobsters in their Season. Pure Cod Liver Oil a Specialty. Poultry and Game in Season : : : : : :

258, 260, 262 Cherry St., Waterbury, Conn.

Telephone 683-2

By the turn of the twentieth century, fresh lobsters could be found inland at places like Fulton Fish Market in Waterbury. *From* New Kirmesse Cookbook.

Simply boiling or steaming a lobster leaves it delicious, in a way not possible with, say, pork, which is one reason its meat is so highly prized. Steaming is the best method and reduces the danger of overcooking, but the intense heat of boiling makes the meat easier to remove from the shell. You'll need a large pot for it and salted water. If you can stand it, use your knife to kill the lobster by stabbing it between the eyes, letting the liquids that emerge drain out. The tomalley remains firmer this way, and it's probably more humane. But most people just take the wriggling crustacean and pop it into the bubbling pot to boil it for about eight minutes for the first pound, adding one to two minutes for each quarter pound after that. Steaming it takes about ten minutes for the first pound, with about forty to forty-five minutes for a five-pound lobster, if you really need the biggest one. You can actually steam a lobster in a microwave, but it takes more work than the stove.

When European settlers first colonized Connecticut, lobsters five to six feet long were caught in the Sound. Once the strange biblical prejudice against these animals was conquered, they quickly became a delicacy on every menu. If a lobster was boiled, it was left to cool and served that way, often with a gravy or mustard and vinegar dressing. Beef and veal gravy were popular for lobster in the early years. Drawn butter was made, according to Catharine Beecher, by rubbing "two teaspoonfuls of flour into a quarter of a pound of butter. Add five tablespoons of cold water. Set it into boiling water and let it melt, and heat until it begins to simmer, and it is done. Never simmer it on coals, as it fries the oil and spoils it." This could be poured over the lobster by itself, mixed with capers or used as a foundation for gravy.

Many made lobster soups or stews. A simple stew was made by sautéing the meat in butter, adding tomalley and stirring in hot milk or cream. A more elaborate soup was made by adding chopped lobster claw meat to egg yolks, butter and seasoning, forming small dumplings.

Simmering any available stock, a chef would add leg meat and roe, creating a pinkish coloring. She would add the dumplings to the soup and cook gently for about five minutes before serving.

Lobster bisque was always a favorite. Today, at Soup Thyme in Monroe, chef Ronald Lee makes dozens of hearty soups for the lunch crowds of Fairfield County. His lobster bisque uses no milk but is a particularly thick, creamy version with hints of garlic and chopped lobster distributed nicely throughout:

Lobster Bisque

1 cup onion

2 garlic cloves

2 tablespoons olive oil

1 cup white wine

¼ stick butter

¼ cup flour

4 cups fish stock

2 cups lobster meat, finely chopped

Salt and pepper

Sauté chopped onion and garlic in olive oil for 10 minutes, then add white wine and cook another 10 minutes before setting aside. In a saucepan, melt butter, add flour and cook 5 minutes, stirring constantly. Add fish stock and stir until a creamy consistency, then add the onion mixture. Add lobster and a pinch of salt and pepper, stirring until blended well. Put in a casserole dish and bake 35 minutes at 400 degrees. This additional step further thickens the bisque and blends the flavors.

Lobster potpie was another popular colonial dish in which lobster meat was mixed with potato, butter, pepper, onion, mushrooms, broth, cream, cornstarch, salt and more. A method that became popular in the 1700s was fricassee, simmering the meat in wine or cream and seasoning. People also used lobster sauce for other dishes, mixing six tablespoons of vinegar, yolks from two boiled eggs, some lobster roe, a spoonful of mustard, two tablespoons of salad oil or melted butter and salt and pepper. And some married Connecticut's oysters and lobsters in a delicious—perhaps too delicious—combination:

Oyster-Stuffed Lobster

2 ounces butter

½ cup onion

½ cup celery

½ cup mushrooms

1 pint oysters with liquor

4 cups bread crumbs

2 tablespoons parsley, chopped

1 teaspoon salt

¼ teaspoon black pepper

½ teaspoon thyme

¼ teaspoon marjoram

4 1-pound to 1½-pound lobsters

Melted butter

Lemon wedges

Sauté chopped onion and celery in butter until soft and then add chopped mushrooms and cook a few more minutes until tender. Open and drain the oysters, saving the liquor. Roughly chop the oysters and put into the onion mixture. Add bread crumbs and spice to the liquor, enough to be absorbed by the bread crumbs until moist. Meanwhile, dispatch the lobsters and split them lengthwise, cracking the claws and removing any unwanted organs. Grill shell side down on a preheated grill or broil for five minutes. Fill the cavity with stuffing and wrap in foil. Place shell side down on the grill or shell side up for the broiler. Broil 15 minutes and serve with melted butter and lemon.

Although many early Americans took lobsters from the Sound to boil or bake, the first commercial fisheries did not appear in Connecticut until the 1800s. New London and Mystic fishermen began a lively trade, especially to New York. They even invented a "lobster smack," a boat with a large, freely circulating tank, to keep the crustaceans alive and fresh until they reached the city. Small coves were turned into "pounds," and later many shoreline eateries and shacks built their own, sometimes right underneath.

This practice led to alternate methods of eating lobster. North of us, the lobster roll was invented: a cold sandwich of lobster pieces and celery smothered in mayonnaise. However, this chicken-salad method was not the way people usually enjoyed the succulent meat of the king of crustaceans. We dipped it hot in butter. So why not create a sandwich that preserved this immortal taste? In 1934, a fish market owner named Harry Perry did just that. His little shop on the Post Road in Milford began to serve the hot buttered meat on French bakery rolls from Stratford. Perry grilled the rolls four at a time, heated the lobster and slathered it in hot butter. Soon, the small fish market had a new sign that read "Home of the Famous Lobster Roll." Other restaurants along the Connecticut coast took the idea and ran with it.

Today, places like Lobster Landing, a one-hundred-year-old fish shack in Clinton, do these summer treats properly, with rolls filled with flesh from claws, legs and tails of lobsters fresh from the Sound and dressed with butter and lemon:

Hot Buttered Lobster Roll
....

1 pound lobster meat
4 large split-top buns
1 stick butter

If you are buying the lobster in the shell, you can crack and pick the meat after steaming very lightly and cooling. If getting the meat frozen from the store, then you will want to let it thaw first. If fresh, it's ready to use. Break up the tail meat into smaller pieces. Use a little bit of the lobster juice, perhaps a tablespoon, to start a simmer in a pot and slowly add butter, one tablespoon at a time, until a nice poaching situation has developed. Do not let it boil. Add the lobster meat, tossing lightly and consistently about 4–5 minutes. Meanwhile, butter and toast or grill the split-top buns. If you would like to make your own split-top New

An early venue for "fast food," seafood shacks like the Lobster Landing in Clinton were found in many coastline towns. *Courtesy of the authors.*

England rolls, see chapter 17. One piece of advice, though: make them large. Lobster Landing uses a small grinder roll and as a result can stuff it with lobster and butter without disintegration. Fill these sturdy toasted buns with succulent, buttery lobster meat and pour the emulsified sauce over them. If you're so inclined, a spritz of lemon juice is all that's needed. Some people add chopped celery, onion or herbs. But other than texture, there is no earthly reason for this.

The key to any of these dishes is respecting the lobster meat, that nearly perfect food from the sea, that rich and creamy delight hidden inside a hard shell. It is one of the best "pure" foods we can eat. And though cracking the shell apart can be fun, enjoying a lobster is also a study in patience and hard work, a meal that must be earned. Though it doesn't seem possible, that work might make an already perfect meal even better.

PART III

Forest and Farm:
Meats

9

On the Wild Side

Today, hunting is a hobby in Connecticut and limited compared to western states or even larger eastern states like Pennsylvania. But for the Algonquian tribes who occupied much of Connecticut, it was necessity. Moreover, since the Algonquians were primarily farmers, killing deer was as much protection for crops as it was for the meat. But it wasn't only deer. The Native Americans in Connecticut hunted nearly everything that moved, including moose, bear, raccoon, opossum, rabbit, squirrel, porcupine, fox, mink, vole, muskrat, beaver and loon. Sometimes hundreds of men would drive wild animals in front of them. Women built temporary hunting camps and fires to smoke the meat. The tribes also burned forests around their homes to encourage the proper habitats for game animals or, in the words of Yale's eighth president, Timothy Dwight, "to produce fresh and sweet pasture for the purpose of alluring deer."

The early colonists were not nearly as adept at this practice, and so one of the first trades that took place was for wild game. In 1644, a doe cost two fathom of wampum and a fawn, one. But just a year later, "venison" was two to two and a half pennies per pound. As Miantonomoh, a Narragansett sachem, said in 1642, "You know, our fathers had plenty of deer and skins, our plains were full of deer, as also our woods, and of turkies [*sic*], and our coves full of fish and fowl. But these English having gotten our land, they with scythes cut down the grass, and with axes fell the trees; their cows and horses eat the grass, and their hogs spoil our clam banks, and we shall all be starved." Once the English settlers grew more powerful and stable, they began regulating the hunting practices of their neighbors, and this was one of the primary issues that led to the seventeenth-century Indian wars.

Birds that we would not think to eat today, from swans to crows, were consumed by native and colonist alike. In a diary from Lyme, Fanny Griswold mentions "owl chowders" as one delicacy. Pheasant, partridge, woodcock, plover, snipe, curlew and quail all made it regularly onto colonial tables. However, by the nineteenth century, most were eating only ducks, geese and turkeys. When international epicure Jean Anthelme Brillat-Savarin visited Hartford at the turn of the nineteenth century, he hunted and shot a wild turkey, along with partridges and squirrels, serving the game to his hosts in mouth-watering French preparations. But this was considered a fine sport rather than everyday practice amongst Connecticut farmers. The exceptions were pigeons, including the huge migratory flocks of passenger pigeons that crossed the state annually, netted and clubbed for the table. The pigeons would be washed; stuffed with salt pork, biscuit, eggs and spice; covered with wine; and stewed for several hours.

Quail and partridges returned to the tables of the wealthy at the turn of the twentieth century. Potted quail was popular, combining the birds with pork in a casserole dish to brown. Adding celery, onion, parsley or whatever was available, you would cover it with stock and simmer until tender, allowing it to cool before serving, as the cold meat of game birds was considered more appetizing. Quail also went well with sherry sauces. A partridge might be wrapped in slices of salt pork, roasted and served with an orange sauce, butter, minced onion, dried tarragon, currant jelly, dry mustard and salt.

Pheasants were introduced to Connecticut in the early 1700s, though before that a grouse called an "American pheasant" lived in the coastal areas of the state. By the time the recipes were written down, though, the European and Asian ring-necked pheasants were the only ones left. A "hunter-style" dish might be done by browning the bird in flour, paprika, salt and pepper. Onions, mushrooms and green peppers were browned in butter, and then wine and tomatoes were stewed with a bay leaf and rosemary. The pheasant was placed in a baking dish drenched in this colonial ragout and baked, covered, for forty-five minutes.

While the whole bird made for fine eating, some preferred to highlight the flavor of individual parts, like the breasts or legs:

Stuffed Pheasant Breasts

4 pheasant breasts, boned

3 tablespoons butter

1 onion

1 teaspoon minced garlic

8 mushrooms, sliced

5 ounces pine nuts

Ground sage

Dried parsley flakes

Dried tarragon

Salt and pepper

1 egg

2 tablespoons milk

¼ cup bread crumbs

3 tablespoons flour

Pound breasts until thin. In a small skillet, melt butter and cook onion, garlic, mushrooms and pine nuts until pine nuts brown. Season with herbs, salt and pepper. Place 2–3 tablespoons of the mixture on each breast and roll, securing with toothpicks. Mix egg and milk in a shallow bowl. In another bowl, combine bread crumbs and flour. Dip rolled breasts in egg mixture and then in bread crumbs. Brown the breasts in butter; place into a baking dish and pour remaining melted butter over them. Cook at 350 for 20 minutes.

Of course, the most popular game bird was the uniquely American turkey. It was nearly always stuffed and roasted, much as we do today. Catharine Beecher instructs us to, after washing the bird inside and out, "take bread crumbs, grated or chopped, about enough to fill the turkey, chop a bit of salt pork, the size of a good egg, and mix it in, with butter, the size of an egg, pepper, salt, and sweet herbs to your taste." She also suggests beating an egg and mixing it in.

Once stuffed and sewed up, with the legs and wings trussed, the turkey was roasted on a spit by the fire. You heated it gradually, away from direct flame, turning it once or twice for fifteen minutes, putting it close to the fire and basting often "with butter on a fork. Dredge it with flour just before taking it up." This helped to

Roaming wild, turkeys were a classic colonial meal, becoming big business in the twentieth century. *Courtesy of the Bridgeport History Center.*

brown it nicely just before the end of cooking. A wild goose might be eaten in much the same way, although sometimes they covered the breast with salt pork, "then a cheesecloth soaked in melted bacon fat or cooking oil," and roasted it a few hours.

The turkeys in Connecticut during colonial times were much larger than the ones we get today, at thirty to forty pounds, and stood three feet tall. However, they were tougher and darker than the ones we eat today, and thus called for gravy or sauce. Lucy Emerson suggests for a sauce to "take a little water, a bit of thyme, an onion, a blade of mace, a little lemon-peel, and an anchovy: boil these together and strain them through a sieve, adding a little melted butter." Lydia Child champions more traditional gravy, putting a pint of flour and water into the baking pan when the meat is set down to roast. "This does very well; but the gravy is better flavored, and looks darker, to shake flour and salt upon the meat." Brown the meat thoroughly, add additional flour and salt and baste with about a pint of hot water. When the meat is almost fully cooked, pour the drippings into a skillet and boil. To thicken if desired, sprinkle a little more flour and then boil again, stirring well. To make it less greasy, skim some of the fat from it before boiling. Save beef fat, pork fat, turkey or goose fat, as it is "as good for shortening as lard." Used scorched flour if you want the gravy to be darker. Catharine Beecher's recipe is similar but suggests using the giblets.

Populations of turkey, geese and duck decreased throughout the 1800s, and they became an import from the American frontier. Game birds dropped out of recipe books and became less important for daily eating, although rich families hired French chefs to cook their pigeons and quail. However, turkey and duck resurged on menus in the 1900s as their domestication became widespread. The following recipe comes from chef Leo Roy at the Old Riverton Inn, the 1796 coaching lodge on the route from Hartford to Albany still in operation today. His delicious traditional preparation takes you back to the stagecoach days of old Connecticut, while still tasting fresh and modern:

Roast Duckling with Black Cherry Sauce

1 roast duckling	Connecticut white wine
½ orange	2 cans northwest pitted bing cherries
½ lemon	1 ounce triple sec or Grand Marnier
½ lime	Chopped parsley

Remove innards from duck, rinse and pat dry. Salt and pepper the duck, stuff with ½ orange, ½ lemon and ½ lime. Set on a rack in a pan and cook for 15–20 minutes at 425 degrees. Reduce heat to 350 and continue to roast 20 minutes per pound, basting with white wine. Flip at 40 minutes, flip again and cook another 60 minutes. Jack up heat and cook 10–20 minutes more if you like a crispy skin. Meanwhile, bring the cherries to a boil, thickening with arrowroot or cornstarch slurry. Add 1 ounce triple sec or Grand Marnier, the zest from the orange and chopped parsley for garnish.

Of course, four-legged game was also found in the state. Bears and beavers regularly disappeared from overhunting, returned and disappeared again. Rabbits and hares had always been popular on the table when they could be caught, and wild hogs were sometimes mentioned but were probably escapees rather than a population of true boars. Snapping turtles abounded "from time immemorial" in the Connecticut River and tributaries, some weighing up to thirty pounds. They were made into soup, similar to the more famous one from Pennsylvania, combined with veal knuckles, chicken fat, onions, carrots, celery, cloves, tomatoes, Madeira, eggs, lemon slices and spices, all in a beef broth. You would simmer the turtle meat first for about an hour while browning the veal knuckles and onions. Making a roux in another pot, you would add the other ingredients and the broth slowly, simmering for three to four hours. After cutting the turtle meat into bite-sized pieces, you would cook it again with the lemon and Madeira and then combine with the eggs and the other pot, adding more wine if necessary. It was always hard work to harvest a turtle and make this soup, "but the rich, robust result is well worth the effort."

However, the only game animal that appears regularly in cookbooks other than turkey and duck is deer. Originally, venison was really a side effect of the extensive need for buckskin. Before cotton became readily available, everyone wore comfortable and long-lasting buckskin pants and shirts. And everyone ate the wonderful deer meat. Minced venison pies were made by the dozen and stacked in the cold pantry to eat throughout the winter. Lucy Emerson says to "raise a high round pie, shred a pound of beef suet, and put it into the bottom; cut your venison in pieces, and season it with pepper and salt. Lay it on the suet, lay on butter, close the pie, and bake it." She notes that meat pies "require a hotter and brisker oven than fruit pies."

Wild game continued to be served in markets and butcher shops long after people stopped hunting for their own tables. *From* New Kirmesse Cookbook.

Venison stew and roast venison were two other popular recipes. For stew, the venison needed to be simmered long enough to make it tender, but not too long. Potatoes, carrots, celery, red wine and an anchovy-based sauce like Worcestershire would be added near the end of the process. A leg was often marinated for several days before roasting. Catharine Beecher recommends making a sauce for this by boiling a half pint of liquor in which the meat cooked and adding pepper, salt, currant jelly and wine to taste, then adding about a teaspoon of scorched flour mixed with a little water.

A variation on stew, and a twist on a favorite comfort dish, is venison chili. This recipe incorporates molasses and a hint of cinnamon for a savory, filling meal:

Venison Molasses Chili

4 ounces bacon, cut into pieces

2 pounds venison meat, cut into bite-sized pieces

1 teaspoon black pepper

½ teaspoon salt

1 large onion

6 garlic cloves, minced

1 teaspoon red pepper flakes

1 teaspoon cayenne pepper

1 teaspoon dried basil

1 teaspoon nutmeg

¼ to ½ teaspoon cinnamon

½ teaspoon dry mustard

1 28-ounce can crushed plum tomatoes

1 tablespoon Worcestershire sauce

⅓ cup molasses

3 cups water

3 ounces tomato paste

4 cups red kidney beans, drained and cooked

In a large pot, cook bacon until fat begins to render. Add venison and season with pepper and salt. Add onion, garlic and red pepper flakes and cook about 10 minutes, until onions are tender and venison browns. Mix in cayenne pepper, basil, nutmeg, cinnamon and mustard. Add tomatoes, Worcestershire sauce and molasses. Dissolve tomato paste in water and add. Bring the mixture to a boil, then reduce heat and simmer for 1 hour. Add beans and simmer until meat is tender, another 30–45 minutes. Add additional water if necessary. Serve with sour cream or grated cheese.

As populations continue to increase in Connecticut and around the world, the types of food we eat will need to expand. Learning to appreciate the subtle flavors of wild game will probably be as necessary for our descendants as it was for our ancestors. The good news is that wild game has reappeared on restaurant menus around the state. We may never again develop a taste or market for owl chowder, but more diversity in our diet will certainly help us face the challenges of the next millennium.

1 0

Mostly Pork

In colonial Connecticut, on a cool October day of a good year, when the rye was reaped and the pumpkins picked, a pig roast would have been the culmination of the harvest, a celebration and preparation for the long winter. First you would salt the slaughtered pig, filling the empty organ cavity with buttered bread and spices. Sliding the spit through the mouth and down the length of the body, you would brace the legs with skewers in the fireplace. Seasoned logs "kindled with charcoal and small sticks" would flame, roasting the pig slowly, fifteen minutes a pound. You would baste it often with butter until it is a "pale brown." Catharine Beecher says that "when the meat is nearly done, the steam from it will be drawn toward the fire." Meanwhile, chopped liver and brains would boil in allspice and butter to make gravy when added to the dripping pan. Then, as Lydia Child writes in *The American Frugal Housewife*, "when the eyes drop out, the pig is done."

Early American families looked forward to a succulent roast pig all year. Only the poorest New Englanders did not eat meat regularly. However, it was always something to treat carefully and devour with reverence. Today, we take the wide availability of fresh, disease-free meat for granted, eating it rare with impunity. A juicy barbecue rib or a tender, pink lamb "lollipop" is gulped down without forethought of infection. But in early colonial times, you had no way of knowing if an animal was safe to eat. So, you would make sure by cooking the heck out of it and serving the result as "spoon-meat" in hashes, stews or soups.

As the colony brought livestock from Europe, corn-fed swine stock increased more quickly than dairy, and a market for it sprang up as early as the 1600s. As the century progressed, more farm animals were killed and salted in the fall, and winter meals often consisted of salted pork or fish, applesauce and pickled vegetables. Larger farms could always kill fresh meat in the winter, especially for a special occasion like Christmas. However, butchering was always a challenge for a family, and the process usually took several days. Sausage making, cleaning tripe and rendering the head and feet of the animal required everyone to participate. They used the entire animal, making dishes like souse: ears and feet boiled until tender, split when cold and lain in a deep dish. Hot vinegar steeped with cloves, peppercorns, nutmeg and salt was added. When cold, the mixture was often fried in lard and then pickled.

Pork became a staple for all people in early Connecticut, an important source of protein and good health. By the 1750s, it was exported and considered by the English to be "far superior" to all others in America, and merchants from Boston or New York who mixed "inferior pork with that of Connecticut" were scorned. These "fat hogs" could weigh "five or six hundred pounds." To salt fatty pork you would "scald coarse salt with water and skim it, till the salt will no longer melt in water." Packing the pork in tight layers, you kept the rind toward the edge of the barrel, salting each layer and then pouring cooled brine to cover. A heavy stone went on top to ensure the pork stayed down. "Look to it once in a while, for the first few weeks, and if the salt has melted, throw in more. This brine, scalded and skimmed every time it is used, will continue good twenty years."

Another method of preservation was rubbing the freshly killed pig with salt and molasses and smoking it. Yet another was to pour goose grease or lard over cooked meat in a stone or earthen pot, sealing it in. Still another was to use layers of salt in the same way, letting the bloody brine drain off and continuing to add dry salt to cure the meat. Of course, meat cured in this way needed to be soaked in water to make it edible.

However, many cooks came up with interesting ways of eating this preserved meat. You could just fry the sliced salt pork after soaking it in hot water, dipping it in beaten egg wash, rolling it in bread crumbs and frying it in hot fat. This could be served with hasty pudding or on mashed potatoes under a creamy ladleful of gravy. Or you could serve it with apples. Lydia Child tells us it "is a favorite dish in the country, but it is seldom seen in the city." You would fry the pork, drain off the fat, slice apples and fry them until "tender and brown," then lay them around the plate, sometimes adding sliced cold potatoes for a more filling dish. And, of course, small pieces of pork were fried crispy and baked with beans.

Though sweet and sour is a combination of flavors that we associate with Asian cuisine, it was well loved by colonial Americans, especially with pork, as in this traditional recipe:

Sweet and Sour Pork

Rib end of pork

1 clove garlic

1 teaspoon rosemary, minced

Salt and pepper

2 cups brown sugar

1 cup cider vinegar

Rub pork with garlic, rosemary, salt and pepper. Roast fat side up in a Dutch oven for 15 minutes in a 450-degree oven. Cook brown sugar at very low heat in a skillet until melted and caramelized, careful not to burn. Stir in vinegar. Reduce oven to 300 and pour off any fat; brush pork with sweet-and-sour mixture and continue to cook uncovered, until tender—about two hours—basting frequently. When tender, pour off extra fat, slice and serve with additional sauce.

Only recently has Connecticut become heavily wooded again, after spending centuries as "sheep country," looking much like modern-day England. *Courtesy of the Bridgeport History Center.*

In the nineteenth century, the population grew dramatically, and the landscape of the state became less forested, until it looked much like modern-day England. Both a cause and effect of this change was a growing popularity in sheep farming. These were wool sheep, but they were, of course, used for food eventually. However, mutton cannot be salted easily in the same way as pork, and so this meat never became a staple in the same way, remaining below 20 percent of the meat diet. As a fairly tough meat, mutton was cooked for long periods of time until tender and used in pies or as "spoon-meat." However, lamb was eaten fresh by wealthier families and on special occasions.

Roast lamb was popular, marinated in mixtures of oil, carrots, celery, onions, peppercorns, wine and whatever else was on hand. Before roasting, additional herbs could be added and then the meat could be roasted on a spit, or later in an oven, and basted with the marinade. One cookbook suggests an excellent sauce for roast lamb: "pick, wash, and shred fine, some fresh mint, put on it a tablespoon of sugar, and four tablespoonsful of vinegar; or chop some hard pickles to the size of capers, and put them to half a pint of melted butter, and a teaspoonful of vinegar." Or a gravy could simply be made from drippings and flour.

Breast of lamb was more popular than it is today, baked in an oven fat side down, covered in various sauces, like one made with dry red wine, water, currant jelly, parsley and marjoram. You would drain the liquid from the lamb, reducing it in a separate saucepan, adding a slurry of flour and water to thicken it. Vinegar, sugar, eggs and cream might have been added to make the sauce. Dill or thyme fresh from the garden was added right before serving.

Leg of lamb was always popular. Here is a recipe adapted from the *New England Cookbook*, with a delicious sauce of saffron and capers. The saffron would have been a prized import, as it is today:

Leg of Lamb with Saffron and Caper Sauce

....

6 tablespoons butter

1 teaspoon salt

2 cloves garlic, mashed

1 teaspoon cayenne

1 lamb leg, 5–6 pounds, boned,
    tied with bones reserved

1 tablespoon cornstarch

3 tablespoons water

½ cup heavy cream

¾ teaspoon leaf saffron

1 bottle capers, drained

Combine butter, salt, garlic and cayenne and rub over the roast. Wrap lamb, along with bones, in foil and refrigerate overnight. Take lamb from the refrigerator and let it stand for 2 hours. Heat the oven to 375 degrees. Put the foil package in a roasting pan, cooking 35 minutes per pound for medium, 45 for well done. Meanwhile, mix cornstarch with water. Take roast from oven and carefully pour off about two cups of liquid. Add cornstarch to these juices, then add cream and saffron followed by capers. When the meat is done, discard bones and carve. Serve with sauce on the side.

Before the twentieth century, beef was not popular in Connecticut, since milk was much more valuable and pigs easier to keep. However, cows were certainly kept in colonial and early American times, and beef was imported by taverns and those who could afford it. Delicacies like beef tripe appeared frequently on restaurant menus, and steaks were served at the best houses. Calves feet or knuckles were used by everyone to make jelly. For lower-quality beef, mincemeat was the go-to preparation. You would combine chopped beef, suet, apples, raisins, currants, lemon peel, cider vinegar, salt, sugar, coffee, cloves, allspice, cinnamon, jelly and more in a large pot, stirring constantly. After cooling, you would add brandy or sherry and store the result in a stone crock. The saved mincemeat could be spooned into pastries as needed.

A popular way to prepare beef in many of the old cookbooks was "alamode," an inaccurate French term used to make it sound elegant. A cook would cut holes in a round of beef and stuff them with a mixture often consisting of pork, butter, bread, eggs, sweet marjoram, sage, parsley, summer savory and perhaps a pounded clove stuck into the sides. Wine would be added, and the beef would be bound tightly in cloth with "20 or 30 yards of twine." The stuffed meat would be placed into a "two pail pot with sticks at the bottom," with two to three quarts of water and a "jill" of wine, cooking for three to four hours, "if the round be large." The idea of the stuffing was to make the often-tough beef tender.

Preserving excess beef was done by corning—"[rubbing] salt plentifully" and then setting it in the cellar for a few days. These corned beefs would often be used for boiled dinners, and the leavings

Top: Scott Beck and Matt Storch at Match in Norwalk create fantastic dishes like these "Carpetbaggers," twists on traditional fried oysters. *Courtesy of Match Restaurant. Photo by Jeff Kaufman.*

Left: Connecticut's historic election cake has many delicious variations, like this one stuffed full of brandy-soaked golden raisins.

Top: Crispy skin is the key to a delicious roast duck, like this one served with cherry sauce from an Old Riverton Inn recipe.

Left: Unlike an apple pie, a tart like this should be eaten immediately, preferably with guests who appreciate its beautiful textured appearance.

Opposite top: Cornmeal slapjacks with maple syrup in the morning light—what could be more appetizing?

Opposite bottom: The Place in Guilford serves up these simple but stunning roasted barbecue hard-shell clams every summer.

Top: A slice of moist apple coffeecake could be breakfast or dessert, but why choose.

Left: The vertically broiled burgers of New Haven's Louis Lunch have been served on toast for over a century and pair well with a local Foxon Park soda.

The presence of squash in every colonial garden meant a steady supply of warm, rich soup throughout the year.

Make sure to use a large, sturdy roll that can stand up to the succulence of mounds of buttered lobster, like this one at Lobster Landing in Clinton.

Clockwise from top left: The recipe for Blackie's famous homemade relish remains a treasured secret, but you can buy a jar at the legendary Cheshire pit stop and try to figure it out.

Clams were used in dozens of dishes in colonial times, not just chowder. A classic clam hash is still served with brown bread at Pat's Kountry Kitchen in Old Saybrook.

Salted and smoked pork was a staple in Connecticut households for centuries, granting flavor to dishes from chowder to baked beans.

Ginger and molasses were popular imports from the Caribbean, and they were often combined to make crisp, spicy gingersnap cookies.

Left: Baked Grape-Nuts give a caramelized texture to the velvety golden custard of this delicious pudding.

Below: Shad roe wrapped in bacon and broiled is an acquired taste but finds thousands of local devotees to its subtle flavors.

Above: Apple-based drinks were standard in Connecticut for hundreds of years, and cocktails like the Cider Car at ZINC in New Haven continue this tradition.

Left: The crimson and purple shades of red flannel hash make it tasty artwork for any table.

Top: Doughnuts have a long tradition in Connecticut households, though today we usually pick them up from the local bakery.

Left: A proper lobster bisque should be creamy and thick and offer lobster in every slurp, like this wonderful example at Soup Thyme in Monroe. *Photo by Ronald Lee.*

Top: The Italian sandwich made its first American appearance in New London, and today Nardelli's colossal version delights the hungriest eaters.

Left: Delectable artisanal Connecticut cheese clings to baked macaroni in a recipe from the Elbow Room in West Hartford.

Left: This buffalo chicken dog from Two Guys One Grill in Wallingford is a great example of the innovative spirit of Connecticut chefs.

Below: Peaches were an important local crop in the early 1800s and enjoyed in pies like this one throughout the year.

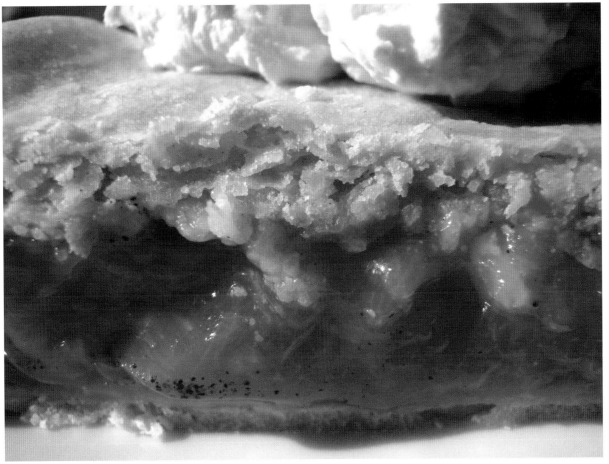

Left: Juicy steamed cheeseburgers, like this one at O'Rourke's Diner in Middletown, are difficult to make at home but well worth the effort.

Below: Shady Glen Dairy Store in Manchester combines two great Connecticut loves: Grape-Nuts pudding and ice cream.

Top: Connecticut loves hot dogs, but no particular style dominates. In New Britain, the famous Capitol Lunch meat sauce is the only condiment you need.

Left: These yummy pecan caramel turtles are given their chocolate shell at Munson's Chocolates factory in Bolton. *Courtesy of Munson's Chocolates*.

Left: These *arepas* at Valencia Luncheria in Norwalk use the traditional Connecticut ingredients of chicken and cornmeal, by way of Venezuela and chef Michael Young. *Courtesy of Valencia Luncheria.*

Below: Frank Pepe's white clam pizza is a Connecticut original, with oregano, garlic, olive oil, pecorino romano and chunks of fresh clams on a thin crust blistered in a coal-fired oven.

Above left: A popular colonial party drink, the frothy punch of syllabub was made from wine, whipped eggs and cream, preferably straight from the cow.

Above right: On a cold winter's day, nothing satisfies like a hearty bowl of venison chili, some artisanal cheese and a local Connecticut brew, like this one from Cavalry Brewing.

Right: Whether you're in love or not, you couldn't find a better gift than a box of Connecticut-made gourmet chocolates like this one from Fascia's in Waterbury.

Left: At Miya's Sushi in New Haven, chef and environmentalist Bun Lai uses invasive species like these Asian shore crabs in a way that makes us rethink our relationship with food.

Below: In Hamden, Mikro's chef Mike Fox reworks the familiar flavors of a Reuben sandwich to showcase pork belly's melt-in-your-mouth succulence, paired here with Cottrell Brewing's Perry's Revenge Ale.

The century-old Filipek's Market in Meriden continues the tradition of great kielbasa making, one of the many contributions from Polish immigrants. *Courtesy of the authors.*

were always eaten in a hash the following morning. The famous "red flannel" hash was invented by the colonists when beets became a popular vegetable. Leftover corned beef and vegetables from a boiled dinner would be reheated the following morning into the ultimate leftover dish. Potatoes were added after the 1730s, replacing turnips or parsnips as the primary complement. The beets "bleed" their red color into the potatoes, turnips or parsnips, and the reddish corned beef completes a striking presentation. Later, the dish became popular with Irish and Polish immigrants, and in the twentieth century it could be found at diners across Connecticut:

Red Flannel Hash

3 potatoes
6 small beets
½ pound corned beef

1 medium onion, diced
Salt, pepper and nutmeg
2 tablespoons bacon fat or butter

Peel and cook potatoes. Dice into small pieces or roughly chop. Peel and dice beets; cook until just tender. Dice corned beef into small "mouthsful-sized" pieces. Combine chopped potatoes, diced beets and onion, but take care not to mash the ingredients. Combine in a bowl; season with salt, pepper and nutmeg. Heat bacon fat (or butter) in a large skillet or frying pan until foaming. Add mixture, pat down and cook over medium heat for about 20 minutes. When the mixture begins to brown, turn slowly and cook evenly for another 10–15 minutes on medium high until mixture is brown and crusty; season as needed with salt, pepper and nutmeg. As Catharine Beecher writes: "There is nothing worse for the health, or for the palate, than a poor hash, while a good hash is not only a favorite dish in most families but an essential article of economy and convenience."

As beef rose in quality and availability in the late 1800s, pork became less popular due to hyped-up "health concerns." Household or farmyard pigs began to be shunned by a wealthier society, and factory workers who did not keep them anyway chose beef. But now in the twenty-first century, pork is making a comeback with many Americans, becoming a staple food in restaurants, with creative chefs finding new and old ways of preparing it. Preparations like salting and smoking have always been ways to take one ingredient, like beef, and change its taste and potential preparation. Pastrami, for example, is made when corned beef, salted in brine, is smoked, resulting in something new. In an innovative twist, chef Mike Fox of Hamden's Mikro riffs on the classic Reuben using pork belly, prepared in brine, rubbed with "pastrami" spices and then smoked. "Classic" never tasted so good:

Pork Belly Reuben

PORK BELLY BRINE

1 quart water
½ cup brown sugar
1 cup kosher salt
1 tablespoon whole black peppercorns
2 teaspoons thyme

3 bay leaves
1 teaspoon whole cloves
6 cloves garlic, crushed
2½ pounds pork belly

In a saucepan, combine water, brown sugar and salt. Bring to a boil, stirring until the salt and sugar are dissolved. Remove from heat and stir in peppercorns, thyme, bay leaves, cloves and garlic. Allow to cool. Place pork belly in a nonreactive container and pour cooled mixture over it. Make sure that the pork belly is completely covered. Cover and refrigerate for 48 hours.

PASTRAMI SPICE RUB

3 tablespoons brown sugar
3 tablespoons chili powder
3 tablespoons kosher salt

¼ cup coarse-butcher ground black peppercorns
3 tablespoons ground toasted coriander seeds
3 tablespoons toasted and ground juniper berries

Prepare smoker for a smoke at about 220 degrees Fahrenheit for 2½ hours. Combine spice rub ingredients. Remove pork belly from brine mixture and rinse under cold water. Pat dry with paper towels and cover with rub. Make sure you press the rub into the surface of the pork belly. Place pork belly in smoker, fat side down, and smoke for 2 to 2½ hours or until it reaches an internal temperature of 165 degrees. Remove from smoker and cool. The pork belly pastrami will continue to gain flavor the longer you let it rest. It can be wrapped tightly and refrigerated for up to one week.

Thousand Island Dressing

1 cup mayonnaise
¼ cup ketchup
2 tablespoons sweet pickle relish
Juice and zest of 1 lemon
Dash of salt and pepper

Mix together ingredients in a small bowl and chill. To assemble the sandwiches, spread dressing onto 2 slices of toasted rye bread; stack 3 slices of Swiss cheese, sauerkraut and pork belly for an exciting variation on the classic Reuben.

In early America, minister, author, Hartford Wit and Yale president Timothy Dwight thought that eating meat two or three times a day was normal, and a breakfast without animal products was "scarcely worth eating." For a farmer or a dockhand or a mother with nine children burning thousands of calories working fifteen hours a day, this meat was essential. Today, we may need it less but love it just the same. Reverend Dwight would certainly have recognized the roots of our meat-loving culture in his own.

1 1

Which Came First?

Most farmers in Connecticut's colonial period bred chickens for egg production, killing them for meat only when too old to produce. Few sold these small birds at market, and they certainly never became an export. Plump young chickens were eaten only by the wealthy, usually roasted and eaten cold, considered a superior method. Amelia Simmons recommends eating only the female chickens, saying, "The female…is preferable to the male, and peculiarly so in the Peacock, which, though beautifully plumaged, is tough, hard, stringy, and untasted, and even indelicious—while the Pea Hen is exactly otherwise, and the queen of all birds." However, "chickens, of either kind [i.e. male and female] are good, and the yellow leg'd the best, and their taste the sweetest."

But chickens were more valuable for eggs, needed for puddings, breads, cakes and more, with recipes often calling for a dozen eggs at one stroke. The egg whites were used as leavening agents in an age when yeast was difficult to keep. Of course, eggs in those days were not as uniform in appearance and quality as today. Amelia Simmons discusses how to pick the best eggs:

> Clear, thin shell'd, longest oval and sharp ends are best; to ascertain whether new or stale—hold to the light, if the white is clear, the yolk regularly in the centre, they are good—but if otherwise, they are stale. The best possible method for ascertaining, is to put them into water, if they lye [sic] on their bilge, they are good and fresh—if they bob up and end they are stale, and if they rise they are addled, proved, and of no use.

Lydia Child gives instructions on how to keep eggs in limewater (calcium hydroxide). To prepare limewater, use a pint of coarse salt and a pint of "unslacked lime" for each pail of water. Too much lime will eat away at the shells. Take care not to crack any eggs, as even one may spoil the whole pail. Cover eggs with limewater and keep in a cool place. While the yolks may redden slightly, she reports that she's seen eggs kept this way "perfectly sweet and fresh" after three years.

To poach an egg, you could break eggs, beat them and "put them on a few coals" with a lump of butter and salt, stirring them until they become thick, and then eat them on buttered toast. Miss Elizabeth Hall of Waterbury at the turn of the twentieth century suggested poached eggs in tomato sauce and serving stewed and strained tomatoes with the eggs. And of course, an omelet was a morning treat. This recipe is adapted from Catharine Beecher, who suggests baking it on coals, which we've left out:

A Very Delicate Omelet

4 eggs, divided

⅓ cup milk

2 teaspoons butter melted into milk

2 teaspoons flour

½ teaspoon salt and ½ teaspoon pepper (to taste)

Ham, thinly sliced or cubed

Green onion, thinly sliced

Mix all except the whites and add those last, beaten until light and frothy. Heat on medium–low in a nonstick frying pan until eggs are almost cooked through. Turn to fold in half and then divide into two servings. As Miss Beecher predicted, the omelet is rather light and fluffy and certainly delicate.

Occasionally, one of the farm's egg-layers would be killed in an emergency. The long boiling and roasting times in older cookbooks reflect the toughness of these birds. Lydia Child gives a recipe for fricasseed chicken that recommends first chopping the chicken into small pieces and then salting, peppering and flouring. Fry in butter until very brown. Remove the meat and make gravy butter with herbs (marjoram or sage), salt and pepper. Once prepared, simmer chicken pieces and onions in the gravy for a half hour, covered.

The bland taste of this overcooked meat led to interesting preparations, one of which was the incredibly popular "chicken smothered with oysters." Amelia Simmons tells us to fill a bird with dry oysters and sew it up. Boil the bird in water, enough to cover, season with salt and pepper and cook until tender. Remove to a deep dish and pour another pint of stewed oysters, which are "well buttered" and seasoned with pepper, over the cooked bird. This fascinating dish remained popular for almost two centuries in Connecticut, but once oysters became more expensive, it went out of style.

Chicken potpie was often the destination of this tougher chicken. Amelia Simmons recommends cutting up six chickens and placing them in a deep-dish pastry, layering in one and a half pounds of butter. Catharine Beecher has a smaller recipe, simmering two chickens in salted water for a half hour. "Line a dish with raised or potato crust, or pie crust," and then layer in chicken with "thin slices of broiled pork" and a hefty tablespoon, "the size of a goose egg," of butter, cut up. Add the boiling liquid, enough to cover, and then add salt and pepper and "dredge a little flour"; cover with a "light, thick crust." Bake for an hour and a half. A variation mixes broiled ham, curry powder and boiled rice with the chicken.

Lydia Child spends the most time with chicken potpie, recommending an earthen or tin pan. She says to make paste with flour, cold water and a little lard. Lay the chicken, a few pieces of salt pork and "a few pieces of your paste here and there; drop an egg or two." Fill the pan with water and add salt and pepper. With lean meat, add some butter or some leftover gravy. Cover with crust and bake a half hour or an hour, depending on the size of the pie. "Some people think this the nicest way of cooking fresh chickens," she says primly. However, more specific directions are probably helpful to enjoy this too-often-maligned dish. The following recipe comes from chef Leo Roy at the Old Riverton Inn:

In the twentieth century, chicken farms appeared all over the state but have mostly disappeared today. *Courtesy of the Bridgeport History Center.*

Chicken Potpie

5- or 6-pound chicken
2½ teaspoons salt
1 cup each of carrots, celery
   and onion, diced
1 bay leaf

2 leaves sage
A few sprinkles of clove powder
1 teaspoon whole peppercorns
½ cup butter
½ cup flour

PASTRY FOR CHICKEN POTPIE

2½ cups flour
1 cup butter
¼ cup shortening

1 teaspoon salt
⅓ cup water

Place bird in stockpot. Add water to cover and 2½ teaspoons salt, the medley of chopped carrots, celery and onions and the bay leaf, parsley, sage, clove powder and peppercorns. Cover and bring to a boil for 1½ hours, depending on size. Reduce heat and simmer until chicken is tender. Check for doneness before removing from pan, or if it's not done enough, return to pan and simmer for longer. Reserve 3 ½ to 4 cups of cooking liquid and vegetables. In a large skillet or saucepan, make a roux with ½ cup butter and ½ cup flour. Cook until slightly browned. Add liquid slowly until a thick gravy is made. Add vegetable and cut-up pieces of chicken; warm through and add more reserved liquid as needed.

Prepare a piecrust with either a pastry fork or food processor. Chill and roll out to ¼-inch thickness. For small personal pies, roll out 4- to 5-inch circles or simply divide it in half and use whatever pie plate you have. Spoon the chicken mixture into prepared crust, put top on and brush with egg wash. Bake a large pie in a 425-degree oven for 25 minutes. For small personal pies, bake 12–15 minutes or until golden brown. Let stand before cutting.

This recipe would work with the tough chickens of yesteryear but is even better with our plumper, juicier "broiler chickens." The chickens first began changing in the nineteenth century with improvements in breeding programs. Barred Plymouth Rock chickens originated in Connecticut in the 1860s, bred by Reverend Upham of Wilsonville. They became popular throughout the nation for both high egg production and meat value. In the early twentieth century, poultry overtook apples and peaches as the state's primary export.

On rural roads, strange farm buildings with long rows of south-facing windows began to appear. These "egg factories" were a new and healthier environment for two million hens. Each would lay between two and three hundred eggs a year, a number that would have staggered an eighteenth-century farmer. This led to hatcheries like Hall Brothers in Wallingford, which produced nine million chicks a year in its incubator rooms. Despite its small size, by World War II, Connecticut produced the fourth most broiler chicks in the country. Hartford poet Wallace Stevens remarked on these chicken farms throughout rural Connecticut as a permanent feature of the landscape.

Throughout the twentieth century, Connecticut continued to pioneer the chicken industry. Frank Saglio emigrated from Italy in 1900, working at Hale's orchards in Glastonbury. In 1917, he bought a farm he later called Arbor Acres. His son Henry began breeding a white-feathered bird due to his annoyance at plucking the black pinfeathers. Then, the nationwide grocery A&P sponsored a competition to find "the chicken of tomorrow." Henry entered in 1948, even though his farm was primarily a cauliflower producer, the largest in Connecticut. His White Rock chickens were judged the second best in the country and the best purebred. After winning again, Arbor Acres began marketing these white-feathered birds across the nation, and by 1958, 50 percent of all chickens consumed in the world came from this Glastonbury farm's stock.

And the Saglios weren't the only pioneers. In the 1940s, Jewish immigrants Alphonsine and Jacques Makowsky fled the Nazis in Europe and settled in northeastern Connecticut on Idle Wild Farm to raise African guinea hens. Then, in the early 1950s, after a fire destroyed their henhouses, they began crossbreeding Cornish gamecocks with various chickens and other birds, including a White Plymouth Rock hen and a Malayan fighting cock. They developed the Cornish game hen, a delicious, all-white-meat bird just big enough for one serving. The Makowskys began selling these at a rate of three thousand per day to fine restaurants like the 21 Club in New York City, and the strain became one of the most popular in history.

As chicken became a more popular export, it also became the backbone of kitchens and restaurants in the state. Chef Michael Young of Valencia Luncheria in Norwalk uses his vast experience in different cuisines to take the Venezuelan *arepas* dish to the next level. This delicious comfort food is great for breakfast, lunch or dinner and showcases one of the new cuisines that are changing Connecticut's culinary landscape:

Chicken Arepas

Arepa Dough

2½ cups warm water

1 teaspoon salt

2 cups fine ground cornmeal

Chicken Tamarillo

4-pound chicken

¼ cup olive oil

1½ Spanish onions, julienned

1 red bell pepper, julienned

1 green bell pepper, julienned

5 garlic cloves, chopped

1 28-ounce can San Marzano whole tomatoes

3 ounces Worchestershire sauce

4 ounces chipotle sauce

1½ tablespoons dry oregano

2 tablespoons Adobo seasoning

Salt and pepper to taste

1 bunch fresh cilantro, chopped

THE QUALITY CHICK WITH THE BRED-IN PROFIT RECORD

HALL'S *Quality* CHICKS

have, for 33 years, contributed importantly to the prosperity of New England farmers. Today, 375 farm families supply our hatcheries with eggs from superior flocks which they manage conscientiously to help us maintain the New England reputation for quality.

HALL BROTHERS HATCHERY, INC.
BOX 50   WALLINGFORD, CONNECTICUT   Tel. 645-J2

Chicken farming became so popular that egg hatcheries like Hall's in Wallingford sprang up to serve the needs of prospective farmers. *Courtesy of the Hamden Historical Society.*

To make the dough, pour water in large bowl, add salt and stir. Slowly add cornmeal (pan harina) while mixing and knead until smooth and firm. Let it rest 10 minutes and then form discs that are ½-inch thick and 5 inches round. These discs can be deep-fried, or they can browned on a hot skillet and finished in the oven. Meanwhile, place the whole chicken in stockpot and cover with water. Bring to a boil, reduce heat and simmer 1 hour, 15 minutes, or until fully cooked. Remove chicken to cutting board and strain and reserve stock. Remove skin and discard. Remove all the meat and shred by pulling apart with your hands. Heat olive oil on medium heat in rondo (or large high-sided skillet) and sauté onions for 10 minutes. Add peppers and garlic and sauté for 5 minutes. Crush tomatoes with hands and add to skillet along with the juice from the can. Add chicken stock and simmer 5 minutes. Add shredded chicken, Worchestershire sauce, chipotle sauce, oregano, Adobo, salt and pepper to taste and simmer another 10 minutes. Fold in cilantro before serving on the folded cornmeal bread.

It's hard to imagine a menu without chickens, but that has only been possible in the last century, in part because of the farmers, scientists and chefs of Connecticut. From the international egg-laying contest begun in Storrs in 1912 to pioneering work controlling poultry diseases like chickenpox, our state has been at the forefront of the chicken revolution. Think about that the next time you take a bite.

PART IV

Culinary Transformations:
Bread, Dairy and Beverages

From Election Cake to
Pepperidge Farm

In pre-Revolutionary Connecticut, election day was not one day in November. Vote counting took place throughout the spring, and in May the formal tally of votes took place in Hartford. Everyone looked forward to making his vote count but also to eating the traditional election cake, which was served to the visiting representatives. There was an election sermon and a procession to the statehouse, and at 2:00 p.m., the assembly convened. At 6:00 p.m., a guard fired a salute. The next evening, after election day, an election ball was held, and cake was served throughout.

This tradition persisted and expanded, and although stories vary, the cake seems to have been baked for most elections, even rural, local ones, into the 1800s and beyond. In 1886, the *Memorial History of Hartford County* says that election day was considered "the reddest-lettered in our calendar," and its celebrations "brightened the whole year." During the whole week, voters would visit neighbors, especially since many farmers had to ride in from rural areas to a voting place. Every housewife needed to have spring cleaning done and election cake baked for the occasion—since so many visitors would be expected. In Connecticut, both democracy and baking were taken very seriously.

Hartford Election Cake was rich bread, often filled with dried fruit and sometimes frosted. An early written recipe came from Amelia Simmons in 1796. Her recipe is for an enormous version, made with thirty quarts of flour, ten pounds of butter, fourteen pounds of sugar, twelve pounds of raisins, three dozen eggs, a pint of wine, a quart of brandy, four ounces of cinnamon, four ounces of coriander seed and three ounces of allspice. Hartford's Mrs. Webster included a recipe in *The Improved Housewife* in 1844 that was only slightly smaller, with two pounds of butter, five of flour, sixteen eggs, a pint of yeast, two and a half pounds of raisins, a gill of rosewater, a gill of brandy, two and a half pounds of sugar, half an ounce of mace, a spoonful of cinnamon and a pint of wine. Catharine Beecher's recipe is close to this, except with far fewer eggs. Here is a modernized version that will leave you with dense, sweet bread. It's moist and not too sugary, with subtle cinnamon notes, and works great for breakfast or dessert:

Election Cake

¼ cup warm water

1 package active dry yeast

¼ cup warm milk

½ cup firmly packed brown sugar

1 cup all-purpose flour

1½ cups golden raisins

¼ cup brandy

¾ cup unsalted butter (softened)

½ cup granulated sugar

2 eggs

¼ cup milk

3 cups all-purpose flour

½ teaspoon salt

½ teaspoon mace

1 teaspoon nutmeg

1 teaspoon cinnamon

To prepare the sponge, pour warm water into a large mixing bowl. Sprinkle yeast and mix. Add milk, brown sugar and flour and mix thoroughly for two minutes until thick. Let this rise for 2 to 24 hours at room temperature, the longer the better. In the meantime, soak raisins (or currants, dried cranberries, etc.) in brandy overnight at room temperature, stirring occasionally. For the dough, combine butter and granulated sugar and mix until creamy. Add eggs and milk and continue to beat 3–5 minutes. Add the prepared sponge a little at a time, mixing lightly each time. Add the soaked fruit. In a separate bowl, combine flour, salt, mace, nutmeg and cinnamon. Alternate cream and flour mixtures, stirring well after each addition. Divide the dough in half and put into greased loaf pans (8½ x 4½ inch). Cover dough with a towel and let it rise for an hour. It will continue to rise once it's in the oven. Preheat oven to 375 and then bake loaves for 50 minutes. Remove from pans and cool. If you'd like to brush the loaves with brandy, it adds a sheen, but it's unnecessary if you're going to add frosting. They get better with time, wrapped and left to stand for two days at room temperature.

Some election cakes included a variety of dried fruit, a sugar-icing drizzle or powdered sugar sprinkled over the top. It all depended on what was available. It was partly this added sweetness that caused essentially a dense bread to be called a cake. These uncertain areas between bread and cake become obvious with "rich tea loaf," flavored with grated lemon peel and lemon extract—a dense white bread. The lemon flavoring gives a delicate richness; cut thick, slices toast nicely served with butter and honey. This was descended from, transformed into or identical to "loaf cake," a sweet bread or cake depending on the source.

But complications were not relegated to a few recipes; the entire bread-versus-cake question goes much deeper. In the centuries before colonization of the Americas, Europeans began to add milk, butter, sugar, spices and especially eggs into their dough. At first, these merely enriched bread, but eggs also provided leavening. This began to change the yeast-raised breads into something different.

Yeast was often obtained by using the dregs from a keg of beer, called the "emptins" by Amelia Simmons. These emptins were collected by methods like this one:

Elizabeth Campbell's Dry Yeast

1 gallon of water and fresh hops
3½ pounds rye flour
7 pounds Indian meal

Boil the hops for ½ hour, then strain. Mix in rye flour and let stand one day in a warm place. Then mix in cornmeal, kneading the resulting dough and rolling it to ½-inch thick. Cut into cakes and leave in the sun to dry. When you need yeast, use these cakes soaked in water overnight near the fire.

You could also add a little molasses to this to give the yeast more to eat. Of course, the use of dried yeast powder and chemical leavenings like "pearl ash" and then baking soda and powder made this process unnecessary. Furthermore, modern pasteurization made the old process of scalding milk unnecessary though unfortunately also made bread less fluffy. These developments helped complete the separation between breads and cakes. Meanwhile, cakes began to be made solely by beating egg whites into foam and folding them into the batter. Nevertheless, during at least a three-century period, the terms "bread" and "cake" seemed interchangeable despite yeast or egg and also varied according to size and shape or author and cook.

In the mid-1800s, Harriet Beecher Stowe said that bread "is the very foundation of a good table" and spent many pages in her essay "Cookery" detailing the ins and outs of proper bread baking, saying it "can be cultivated to any extent as a fine art." She outlined four methods of making bread: fermentation, effervescence of acid and alkali, egg and gaseous pressure. Stowe also detailed the "salt-rising" bread process, which mixed flour, milk and salt and left them to ferment. However, this process had an "unmistakable smell" that caused many cooks to "pause before consummating a nearer acquaintance." The use of acid and alkali substances like sour milk and saleratus (baking soda) to form carbonic acid gas was very popular, she writes, but difficult to achieve a balance with. She laments the loss of the "respectable mode of yeast brewing" that made such a balancing act necessary. "Good patriots ought not to be put off in that way," she claims, and anything less than the finest bread is "wholly unworthy of the men and women of the Republic."

Bread making in brick beehive ovens was standard in colonial America. The average oven was forty inches deep and held "ten or twelve pie plates." In the 1820s, these beehive ovens were improved with cast-iron doors that had adjustable "baffles," allowing the baker a modest control over oxygen and heat. Once a week, the iron door was opened to feed a fire of dry wood, which heated the bricks. Then it was swept out and the chimney closed, and the bread was thrust inside on a large pan or sometimes a bed of cabbage or oak leaves.

The first breads were made with corn, but when the colonists introduced rye flour from Europe, they were often mixed, resulting in brown or "Ryaninjun" bread, which became the bread of the majority. Lydia Child writes, "Some people like one third Indian in their flour. Others like one third rye; and some think the nicest of all bread is one third Indian, one third rye, and one third flour…A mixture of other grains is economical when flour is high." The following recipe is modified from hers:

Ryaninjun Bread

....

1 teaspoon salt

2¾ cups cornmeal

2 cups water, split

2 packages yeast, divided

¼–⅓ cup brown sugar

2¾ cups rye flour (plus more as
    needed for kneading)

Harriet Beecher Stowe's worldwide success as a novelist led to collaboration with her sister, Catharine, who far surpassed her in contributions to food and domestic affairs.

Sprinkle salt over cornmeal. Add a cup (or more) of boiling water and mix in a separate bowl. Cool the remaining 1 cup of water to lukewarm, sprinkle yeast and dissolve. Add brown sugar. Combine cornmeal mix and yeast mixture and gradually add rye flour. Mix well with a wooden spoon (or in a food processor) until a mound forms. It may be slightly wet. Turn onto floured surface and add rye flour until it is no longer wet and can be kneaded. Place in a greased bowl and cover. Let rise in a warm spot for about 1 hour. Punch down, divide in half, knead each half slightly and form into loaves. Let rise again. Put in greased loaf pans; let rise again about 40 minutes. Cook in a 375-degree oven for 35–40 minutes, until slightly browned, light almond in color and crinkled on top. The heavy grain will prevent this bread from rising too much, leaving a dense but fairly moist loaf. You can see the texture of both the cornmeal and the rye flour. It is excellent as toast with butter and honey and good cubed in fish chowder.

Wheat was rare because it did not grow well in the rocky ground. But there were exceptions, like Pleasant Valley in North Lyme, which had good soil. In 1717, these fields were producing enough to export to Boston. Ryaninjun began to be made with Child's recommendation of one-third rye, one-third cornmeal and one-third white flour. Corn was dropped when possible, leaving bread made with white and rye. The *Early American Cookbook* by Hyla O'Connor includes a recipe made with five cups white flour, four cups rye flour, two cups milk, one tablespoon salt, one-third cup dark molasses, one-fourth cup butter, one and one-fourth cups warm ale, two packages active dry yeast and a half teaspoon caraway or fennel seeds. Baked for thirty-five minutes in a 375-degree oven, this will make two loaves of bread, hearty but not too dense, with a light brunette color given by molasses.

Ryaninjun bread, one of the most popular recipes of colonial times, combines cornmeal and rye flour for a hearty loaf with a dense and beautiful texture. *Courtesy of the authors.*

As wheat and "white" flour became more and more available through trade, breads like "Anadama" developed in New England, still using a little cornmeal but mostly white flour. The cornmeal doesn't offer much flavor but deepens the texture, making this perfect for toast:

Anadama Bread

7–8 cups all-purpose flour
1¼ cups yellow cornmeal
2½ teaspoons salt
2 packages active dry yeast

⅓ cup butter, softened
⅔ cup room-temperature molasses
2½ cups warm tap water

Combine 2½ cups flour with cornmeal, salt and yeast in a large bowl. Add butter and molasses. Add water slowly and beat 2 minutes. Add remaining flour ½ cup at a time and mix with electric beater until stiff. Then add remaining flour and stir into a stiff dough. Knead on a floured surface about 10 minutes. Let rise in a greased bowl, covered in a warm place, until doubled—1 hour. Grease two 9x5 bread pans. Punch down dough when doubled, divide, shape into loaves and place in pans. Cover and let rise again, another 45 minutes, until doubled; meanwhile, preheat oven to 375. Bake for 45 minutes until golden.

In the nineteenth century, bread moved out of the province of individual cooks and became an industry. Connecticut has been a pioneer in this business since 1818, when Benjamin

Gilbert, a local tanner and currier, invented the horsehair sieve, leading to the first lumpless flour. The sieve was essential for all bakers until pre-sifted flour came out in the twentieth century. Following him was Reverend Sylvester Graham of Suffield, who became a dietary reformer in the 1800s, emphasizing vegetarianism and improved eating habits. In 1829, he invented Graham bread, made from un-sifted flour without chemical additives like alum and chlorine, popular at the time to make bread white. His belief in whole-wheat flour and its benefits was visionary.

As the 1800s progressed and the cities in Connecticut grew, residents there relied more and more on commercial bakeries, which produced breads, cakes and other confections. Companies like Frisbie Pies pioneered the industry by creating what were probably the first mass-produced pies in the world. This mass production was later used to bake the pre-sliced breads that dominated twentieth-century groceries, some of them also pioneered here.

In 1937, on a small farm in Fairfield, thirty-nine-year-old Margaret Fogarty Rudkin baked bread for her son, who suffered allergies. The doctor treating him liked the bread so much that he ordered some for his other patients. On the strength of this, Rudkin sold some to local grocers, who sold it for twenty-five cents a loaf. Months passed, and Rudkin had to expand her kitchen, eventually moving into a large building in Norwalk. She named her new company after a pepperidge tree on her property. In 1961, she sold the company to Campbell Soup for a cool $28 million, but it is still located in the state, north of Hartford in Bloomfield. It continues to make tasty bread, along with popular products like Goldfish crackers.

Pepperidge Farm is not the only important company to grow out of the rich bread-making tradition of Connecticut. Dean and Betty Arnold of Stamford began baking bread in 1940, using high-quality ingredients and developing a rich, golden loaf. In Greenwich in the 1960s, they built the largest bakery under one roof in the world and continue to make some of the best sliced breads in America.

Harry Lender was another innovator, emigrating from Poland in 1927, buying his first bakery in New Haven for $600 in 1929. He focused on the bagels popular with other immigrants from Eastern Europe and elsewhere. By 1934, he had sold enough to move into a larger bakery, and by the 1950s, his bagels were in such demand that a new method was needed. He experimented and perfected a method of freezing bagels to spread the baking throughout the week. He also pioneered pre-slicing and packing the bagels in polyethylene bags to keep them fresh. Then, with the rise of grocery stores, the Lender family began to distribute these frozen bagels in supermarket aisles. Lender's Bagels became the most popular of all time.

Lyman Beecher's remembrance of Revolutionary-era food included "rye bread, fresh butter, buckwheat cakes, and pie for breakfast." This bread-heavy diet is only possible through culinary methods handed down from cook to cook over centuries. Abolitionist, women's rights advocate and food writer Lydia Child once said, "It is more difficult to give rules for making bread than for anything else; it depends so much on judgment and experience." In that way, the tradition of celebrating our election days with rich, frosted bread was the perfect reminder for early Americans not to take their democracy for granted, despite its many foibles and frustrations. Child could have been speaking of either bread or elections when she said, "In these things, I believe wisdom must be gained by a few mistakes."

1 3

From the Creamery

Today, you can get fresh Connecticut milk from the refrigerator aisle of any grocery store. Better yet, it doesn't need to be "scalded" before being drunk. This is something we take completely for granted in the twenty-first century. But until recently, fresh milk was available only to those who had a family cow, and even then it was a lot of work. Cows needed to be milked twice daily, and the milk would be used immediately as a cream sauce for a variety of dishes, in breads and cakes and in simple treats like milk porridge. This dish was created by boiling new milk and stirring in flour, then seasoning with salt and sometimes nutmeg and sugar. If you could not use milk right away, it needed to be transformed into butter or cheese for storage. Butter churning was the most common, but when extra milk was obtained, beginning in June, it was processed into cheese. Both activities needed a cool room, and in larger houses, there was usually a separate room called the "creamery" or "cheese room" for these purposes.

Lydia Child gave explicit instructions for these methods, telling cooks to cover any surplus of cheese with paper, "fastened on with flour paste" to prevent exposure to air. Stored in a cool, dry place in earthen tins, you could keep the cheese free from insects for years. Butter would keep if stored in a "clean, scalded firkin, [covered] with strong brine," with a cloth spread over the top. She recommended doing it in September or June, when it would not be "rendered bitter by frost." If the cream was scalded first, then strained and kept one night in the cellar to "get perfectly cold" before using, it gave the butter "a peculiar hardness and sweetness."

Author Harriet Beecher Stowe pointed out that butter in America was usually salted, yellow and hard, without the particles of buttermilk that accrued in the European equivalent. After lamenting bad butter, she said, "The process of making good butter is a very simple one. To keep the cream in a perfectly pure, cool atmosphere, to churn while it is yet sweet, to work out the buttermilk thoroughly, and to add salt with such discretion as not to ruin the fine delicate flavor of the fresh cream." Though well-churned, flavorful butter needs little improvement, a resourceful cook might create rose butter by layering rose leaves and butter in a glass jar to give additional creaminess to dishes that called for rosewater.

A centrifugal cream separator that "can be turned by one who is seated" promised ease and comfort for homemakers. *Courtesy of Hamden Historical Society.*

Cheese also became popular in Connecticut during colonial times. Milk was placed on the fire to warm and curdle and then the curds were broken in the cheese basket, shaped and pressed and put on cheese ladders in the pantry, to be turned over daily. Ezra Stiles, president of Yale during the Revolution, claimed that a pound of cheese was eaten per day in his house. Under "simple remedies," Lydia Child recommends "a good quantity of old cheese" to eat when "distressed by eating too much fruit, or oppressed with any kind of food."

In 1792, Alexander Norton of Goshen began a successful cheese-making operation. At first, he used casks to export this popular cheese but then invented round boxes to ship it, the first time this was done in America. By 1845, over 2 million pounds of cheese were being made in Litchfield County and almost 1 million in Windham. Goshen alone produced 400,000 pounds. In the summer of 1840, milk sold at a retail of five cents, cheaper if you got it at the farm. By this time, millions of pounds of butter were also being produced, and cheese from western Connecticut was renowned throughout America. This led to the "creamery system." The Farmington Creamery was a joint stock company in 1869, and cooperative creameries were popular for twenty years, until competition from huge farms out west shattered local industry.

Cheese was most often eaten by itself or melted on toast. Sometimes it was mixed with egg and baked in ramekins or made into croquettes with flour, egg and salt and fried in lard. Dipping stale bread into melted cheese certainly went on in Connecticut farmhouses, though it was not called "fondue" until well into the twentieth century. The American favorite of macaroni and cheese did not become popular until then, either, after Italian immigrants brought their famous pastas to the state. The following recipe comes from the Elbow Room in West Hartford and is rated by the *New York Times* and Connecticut gourmets as one of the all-time best:

Elbow Room Mac and Cheese
....

1 pint (half a pound) of Cavatappi pasta
1½ tablespoons butter
1 tablespoon flour
1 cup milk
3 ounces half and half
½ cup each of Swiss, cheddar, parmesan and Monterey Jack cheese

Cook the Cavatappi in boiling water with a pinch of salt until tender, 8–10 minutes. Make Béchamel sauce by melting butter in a saucepan, adding flour and cooking until blended. Add milk slowly to thicken. Melt cheese into sauce until smooth. In a baking dish, combine Cavatappi and cheese sauce; stir until pasta is coated. Bake in a 350-degree oven for 40 minutes. The cheeses combine for a creamy, full flavor. Swiss and cheddar provide a bit of sharpness, nicely balanced with the savory Jack and parmesan.

In the mid-1800s, people in Connecticut also began to pay attention to breeding their cows. Devon cows had been popular since colonial times, and Shorthorn and Holstein cows were the most frequently used for dairy. Then, in 1875, a dairy Experiment Station was founded at Wesleyan, later moving to the growing University of Connecticut at Storrs. Jersey cows came into Storrs in 1896, growing into the finest herd of its kind in the country.

As pasteurization methods became popular and improved throughout the nineteenth century, milk and cream were drunk more often without scalding. One popular way to drink these in early America was to make a beverage simply called "cream" that used sweetened cream seasoned with nutmeg, orange or rosewater and a spoonful of wine. You could also whip egg whites and stir this into the cream, heating it over the fire until thick. The juice of lemons or raspberries was substituted for wine in temperance households. Cream and sugar were also mixed to make "whipt cream," like this one:

A Whipt Cream
....

8 egg whites
1 quart cream
½ pint white wine
½ cup sugar

Beat the egg white with the cream, wine and sugar. You could "perfume it (if you please) with musk or Amber gum tied in a rag and steeped a little in the cream." This is more of a meringue than what we think of as whipped cream, which is not made with eggs and is usually flavored with vanilla extract, not wine. Nineteenth-century epicures simply spooned this from glasses. But you can also put it on top of pies, where it works surprisingly well.

Artificial breeding was well established by the twentieth century, and Connecticut's dairy cows averaged 5,780 pounds of milk annually, an astounding 1,205 pounds greater than the U.S. average. Osbornedale Farm in Derby produced a Holstein herd that Waldo Kellogg studied and rated as producing the best milk in America for children and "delicate" adults. This sort of specialization was necessary for Connecticut farms in order to compete with large farms of the American West.

Although ice cream had been made for centuries, the wide availability of iceboxes and refrigerators in the twentieth century made ice cream an omnipresent treat. Waterbury's *New Kirmesse Cookbook* gives a recipe for "Biscuit Ice Cream" with three-quarters cup of sugar, three-quarters cup of water, five eggs (yolks only), one quart of cream, four teaspoons of maraschino, two teaspoons of rum and a pinch of salt. Boil sugar and water to the threads. Beat the eggs thoroughly and pour onto them the hot syrup in a small stream, beating all the while. Place the bowl or saucepan in boiling water and cook for ten minutes, beating all the time with eggbeater. Remove from fire and set into cold water, beating at intervals until cold. Have cream whipped with eggbeater (not churn); stir it gently into the eggs. Flavor and pack as for mousse. Must stand at least four hours.

Not everyone wanted to or could make ice cream at home. By 1925, there were at least twenty ice cream factories in Connecticut, mostly on dairy farms. Finding the right level of butterfat is essential, though. Occasionally, you might stop at a farm (in some other state, of course) that has gotten a little too excited about making the "richest" ice cream around. The result is often oily and unappetizing, leaving a strange feeling in your mouth.

Today, J. Foster Ice Cream in Simsbury has taken classic ingredients of Connecticut's past and created Bacon Maple Ice Cream. Although its recipe is proprietary, here's a similar one that you might try, though you'll need an ice cream maker:

Commercial dairy farming took off at the end of the nineteenth century, helped by UCONN's agricultural program. *Courtesy of the Bridgeport History Center.*

Maple Bacon Ice Cream
....

3 slices bacon
1½ cups heavy cream
⅓ cup maple syrup
1 teaspoon vanilla

Fry the bacon on the stove, pat dry and chop into bacon bits. Put the other ingredients into a blender and mix. Then turn on the ice cream maker and slowly pour the ingredients through the top. Let it start to solidify, about five minutes, and then add the bacon bits. Transfer to a container and let it set in the freezer.

Connecticut became part of the long history of milk preservation when Gail Borden patented the process of condensing milk by vacuum, opening a condensery in Wolcottville in 1856 and again in Burrville in 1857. Although his factory only lasted a few years, it began a worldwide industry that continues long after the original need had disappeared. Why? Because condensed milk tastes so good. And so does butter, and especially cheese, which continues to be made at small Connecticut farms, like Cato Corner in Brooklyn. Its Black Ledge Blue, Brigid's Abbey and Bloomsday cheeses are delicious reminders that milk "preservation" was never just about keeping a valuable resource but also about the wonderful tastes and flavors that arise from our creative methods.

1 4

Let It Brew

At sunset, after twelve hours working in the fields or factory, a man might want something a little stronger than the hard apple cider he drank for breakfast and lunch. The local tavern was only two miles away, and he eagerly hurried there. Perhaps he would splurge for a mug of hot flip, which the tavern keeper would make by taking a very large mug or pitcher "filled two thirds full of strong beer; sweetened with sugar, molasses, or dried pumpkin…and flavored with a dash of New England rum." He might mix in cream or eggs. Then he would shove a red-hot poker, called a loggerhead, into the mixture. This would give a burnt taste and froth and bubble the liquid to the top of the mug. Meanwhile, at home, the hardworking man's wife might be opening a jar of homemade raspberry cordial, while the gaggle of children imbibed freely from a jug of cider, the mild alcohol sending them to bed early without wasting the beef tallow candles.

This was not some exaggerated scene out of an anti-alcohol propaganda pamphlet; it was daily life for nearly every citizen of Connecticut. Of course, daily habits like this did inspire the temperance movements of the nineteenth century and the Eighteenth Amendment to the Constitution that followed. But the everyday practice of consuming alcoholic or boiled beverages was not born out of sloth or unhappiness or addiction. It was considered the healthy thing to do. Wells or streams were often unreliable, and thus processed drinks were a way to keep fit.

As soon as the three colonies of Connecticut were settled, people began finding ways to ferment beverages. At first, home breweries were established to make ale, but English grains did not grow well, and corn was too important as a food source. Homemade wines were made from wild grapes previously cultivated by local Indian tribes. Sack was imported for the first few decades, until colonists made their own sweet wine from grapes and other fruit. Sweet wine was added to a mixture of sugar, nutmeg, eggs and milk to make sack-posset, a drink popular at weddings. Whether the wine was made in Connecticut or imported, it was often mulled and drunk hot, with generous shavings of nutmeg. And of course, when apple trees flourished, cider became the drink of choice for grieving widows at their husbands' funerals, for ordinations and church raisings and for infants at christenings. Yale students drank it at meals, in large tankards that were passed down the common table.

When trade with the Caribbean flourished, "rumbullion" or "kill-devil" began to make an appearance throughout the state. Molasses and "poor sugar" were also imported and distilled as rum on-site in Connecticut as early as the 1680s. The liquor did not travel well from the Caribbean, and this method made much more sense—and profit—to the entrepreneurial merchants of Connecticut. In fact, this became so popular that towns like New London began exporting rum to Europe and Africa, even though they didn't grow the sugar cane. This

Beer did not gain popularity in Connecticut until the urban population rose at the end of the nineteenth century. Before then, cider was king. *Courtesy of the Bridgeport History Center.*

operation became part of the infamous "triangle trade" for slaves. The cost of distillation in the early 1700s averaged around fifteen shillings for one hundred gallons. In the Caribbean, distilling was more troublesome than in our northern climate. Therefore, Connecticut rum soon became famous and lauded across the Atlantic.

Author Lydia Child extolled the virtues of rum in a different way. In her cookbook, dedicated to "those who are not ashamed of economy," she suggested, "New England rum, constantly used to wash the hair, keeps it very clean, and free from disease, and promotes its growth a great deal more than Macassar oil. Brandy is very strengthening to the roots of the hair, but it has a hot, drying tendency, which N.E. rum has not." Most, however, used it for mixed drinks. Hot buttered rum was made by blending rum with brown sugar or maple syrup, butter, cinnamon, grated nutmeg and boiling water. This drink comforted many on long winter nights. Rum mixed with molasses was called blackstrap, a drink thought "barbaric" by all but its devotees. Combining rum and cider also became popular; as the two primary drinks of the state, it was a natural, if somewhat unpleasant, drink called a "stone wall." P.T. Barnum called it "gumption."

The more complicated flip was mostly a tavern drink, though some homes had their own "loggerhead," sometimes called a "flip-dog" or "hottle," which would be heated in the fire and then plunged into the mixture. In 1704's *New England Almanac*, we already see flip as the treasured winter beverage. George Washington's second in command, General Israel Putnam, or "Old Put" to his friends and neighbors in Connecticut, had his own recipe. John Trumbull, celebrated Hartford Wit and nephew of the Revolutionary governor, associated flip with the new nation when he wrote in 1776:

> *While briskly to each patriot lip*
> *Walks eager round the inspiring flip:*
> *Delicious draught! Whose powers inherit*
> *The quintessence of public spirit.*

At an early American tavern, a mug of flip could cost three times as much as your lodging and a little more than your meal. Today, you should find it much cheaper to prepare, though still quite complicated:

Hot Flip
....

4 egg yolks
¼ cup sugar
1 teaspoon nutmeg, grated
½ cup dark rum
1 quart ale

In a mixing bowl, combine yolks and sugar and beat well until thick. Add nutmeg and rum and beat. Pour into a pitcher. Heat ale and then pour into another pitcher. Add ale a little at a time to the egg mixture and stir vigorously—this prevents curdling. Pour contents back and forth into alternating pitchers until frothy and blended. Serve with grated nutmeg. This version is much less bitter than the one that would have been served at the time but is still an acquired taste.

Of course, rum was not the only drink available to early Americans, though it was likely the strongest. Fruit wine and cordials became popular as soon as sugar was widely available, and housewives would make it from whatever was at hand: raspberries, huckleberries, currants and, of course, grapes. Taverns also served apple brandy, cherry rum and a sort of honey wine with spices called metheglin. Wealthier people imported sweet wine from the Canary Islands and Portugal.

The word "cocktail" was not used in America until the mid-1800s, even though the concept was as old as time itself. Punch was a popular version of this. The word comes from the

Hindustani word *panch*, meaning "five," the number of ingredients used at the time. However, the New England punch varied in components, although it was still served in large bowls. Connecticut punches were often made with imported citrus fruits, rum or brandy, water, sugar and nutmeg. But almost anything would do, depending on the tastes of the mixer and available ingredients. Descendant of P.T. Barnum Elisabeth Seeley gave a recipe for "Famous Punch," which included a pint of strong tea, a pint of brandy, a quart of rum, a goblet of Curacao, the rinds and juice of six lemons and oranges, sugar to taste and four quarts of champagne.

Connecticut's own Mark Twain loved "cocktails," especially while smoking his cigars, and he even recorded a recipe for a tropical drink that he imbibed liberally on his sea voyages from New York to San Francisco that included three-quarters pound of sugar, one and a half pounds of ice, a dozen limes, one lemon, one orange and half a bottle of brandy. In 1853, Professor A.C. Twining of Yale invented the first artificial ice-making machine, making cold cocktails possible and popular. Then, in 1892, G.F. Heublein of Hartford created the world's first bottled cocktails, making it easier for those without bartending skills or patience.

Another favorite was syllabub. This frothy milk-based punch was often considered a "ladies' drink" because of its sweetness and was served at Christmastime—as dessert if thick, as a drink if thinner. Though fancy in presentation, the preparation of syllabub was unadorned, if the barn was close by. Amelia Simmons says, "To make a fine syllabub from the Cow, sweeten a quart of cyder [*sic*] with double refined sugar, grate nutmeg into it, then milk your cow into your liquor, when you have thus added what quantity of milk you think proper, pour half a pint or more, in proportion to the quantity of syllabub you make, of the sweetest cream you can get all over it." Some syllabub recipes called for wine and brandy, and a similar drink, made with sherry instead of wine, was called posset. Today, our milk and cream are much thinner, and thus the recipe is slightly altered:

Whipt Syllabub

1 cup white wine
Lemon or orange peel, grated
½ cup sugar
1½ cups milk

1 cup heavy cream
1 egg white
3 tablespoons sugar
Nutmeg

Combine wine, peel and sugar. Stir to dissolve the sugar. Add milk and cream. Beat with an eggbeater until frothy. Clean off beater and beat egg whites separately until stiff; gradually add sugar until peaks form. Pour wine mixture into glasses, top with a spoonful of egg froth. Garnish with citrus rind and nutmeg.

In colonial and post-colonial times, beer was considered "a good family drink," made at home by throwing a handful of hops in a pail of water along with molasses, boiling the mixture and leaving it to ferment with a pint of yeast. Spruce or malt was often added, as well as whatever herbs were on hand. Lydia Child tells us that "if your family is large the beer will be drunk rapidly, it may well remain in the barrel; but if your family be small," bottle it. Throw in a raw potato when the ingredients boil, as it "is said to make beer spirited." If it becomes sour, "it may be used to advantage for pancakes and fritters. If very sour indeed, put a pint of molasses and water to it, and, two or three days after, put half a pint of vinegar, and in ten days it will be the first rate vinegar."

Beer became hugely popular at the end of the nineteenth century amongst city folk, who didn't have access to their own grove of apple trees. When the trees were wiped out by scale in 1904, the number of breweries and wineries skyrocketed. Immigrants from southern Europe planted vineyards on the hillsides and made deep red wines. Along with the usual ingredients, beer was also made from spruce, birch and sassafras, as well as other herbs and roots. Some even made it from pumpkins or parsnips. Ginger beer was popular and was made by combining a cup of ginger, a pint of molasses, a pail and a half of water and a cup of "lively yeast." You scalded the ginger in half a pail of water and then filled the pail with cold water. Yeast was not added until the mix was cold, and the result was bottled.

Water-based beverages were consumed if boiled. Some simply flavored hot water with ginger and molasses, a drink that was called "beverige" after the ancient Roman drink made from vinegar and water. This was called "switchel" if you added rum. Imported coffee and tea were, of course, popular, though large quantities were not brought in until the eighteenth century. And when tea went out of fashion with the Revolution, coffee became the national drink. Nevertheless, it remained a fairly expensive import, with elaborate rituals for roasting, grinding and boiling detailed in various cookbooks. Lydia Child mentions

Operating for over one hundred years, the Diamond Beverage Corporation of Waterbury was one of dozens of local soda and beer brewers in the state. *Courtesy of the Bridgeport History Center.*

that "a bit of fish-skin as big as a ninepence, thrown into coffee while it is boiling, tends to make it clear," though she cautions, "Wash the skin and dry it." She also suggests adding "the white of eggs," "egg shells" or "sweet butter…just before it is done roasting." As for the many coffee substitutes that existed in her day, "none of these are very good," and "the best economy is to go without."

Nonalcoholic sodas became popular in the early twentieth century, with hundreds of small producers all over the state. Today, only a few remain, like Avery's Soda in New Britain, Castle Beverages in Ansonia, Foxon Park in East Haven and Hosmer Mountain Bottling Company in Willimantic. Avery's colorful sodas often come with playful names like Swamp Juice or Lime Ricky and are made with real cane sugar and natural well water. And Hosmer's "dangerous" ginger beer harkens back to the old favorite of Connecticut's merchant fleet.

Today, we can get any tea, coffee or alcoholic beverage from around the world. But at the same time, we have begun turning to local wineries, distilleries and breweries for our own particular flavors. Bartenders and mixologists around the state are experimenting with new possibilities and reimagining the old. In New Haven, co-owners of ZINC Donna Curran and chef Denise Appel are committed to a sustainable, farm-to-table menu that celebrates the surrounding community. Their drinks are no different, and they use brandy from Connecticut's Westford Hill Distillery in a variation on a sidecar, a bold new classic with traditional flavors:

Cider Car
....

1½ ounces New World Aged Apple Brandy

2 ounces apple cider (from Bishops or Lyman Orchards)

½ ounce triple sec

¼ ounce lemon juice

The apple cider should be reduced in a pan with cinnamon sticks about five minutes, but don't reduce it too much or it will become a syrup, making the drink too sweet and thick. When done, mix all of the ingredients together in a martini shaker and agitate for 30–40 seconds. Strain into a martini glass and serve with a lemon twist. Its deep caramel color matches the rich appley flavor.

Today, we no longer have to worry about water quality, but our beverage choices are still determined by taste, health, circumstance and location. And luckily, we still do not need to go far to quench our thirst. Whether we toast with a glass of Connecticut wine or a locally made soda, at the bar or at home, the legacy the early inhabitants bestowed on our drinking habits is a satisfying one.

PART V

The Wholly American Trinity:
Hamburgers, Pizza and Hot Dogs

The Quick Lunch Room

In his poem "Dinner in a Quick Lunch Room," Yale graduate and Pulitzer Prize–winner Stephen Vincent Benet rails against "fast food," writing that "soup should be heralded with a mellow horn" and "over the salad let the woodwinds moan," while instead he hears "clang! crash! bang!" while he broods and gorges "the sticky mess these fools call food!" Written in the early twentieth century, Benet's sentiments foreshadow the spread of fast-food chains across the American landscape, degrading even further the meals that the poet thought should be accompanied by a symphony.

However, "fast" food can be good food, despite the lack of symphonic accompaniment, and it is something that Connecticut has done right, the same way fine dining is done right, by the loving care of chefs and the ingenuity of pioneers. The first fast foods in the state came from the ubiquitous lunch carts that waited for factory workers to emerge from their labor, and the first diner in Connecticut was probably Skee's in Torrington, now sadly defunct. The oldest remaining one is Collin's Diner in Canaan.

One of the foods that developed in the quick lunch room, and perhaps the quintessential American food, is the hamburger. This evolved from the very common dish of ground meat. Here's Hannah Glasse's 1758 recipe from *Art of Cookery Made Plain and Easy*:

> Take a pound of Beef, mince it very small, with half a Pound of the best Suet; then mix three Quarters of a Pound of Suet cut in large Pieces; then season it with Pepper, Cloves, Nutmeg, a great quantity of Garlic cut small, some white Wine Vinegar, some Bay Salt, a Glass of red Wine, and one of Rum; mix all these very well together, then take the largest Gut you can find, stuff it very tight; then hang it up a Chimney, and smoke it with Sawdust for a Week or ten Days;

hang them in the Air, till they are dry, and they will keep a Year. They are very good boiled in Peas Porridge, and roasted with toasted Bread under it, or in an Amlet.

Of course, this has more in common with a sausage than a hamburger. The nineteenth century was full of hamburger-like inventions, with chopped up meat from the poorer beef cuts mixed with onions, egg, spices and other options. Mostly what we call "meatloaf" or "meat cake" was the ultimate goal of this ground meat, and one of the most famous places for this chopped meat was Hamburg, Germany. This was a very popular port city for European immigrants heading to the United States, although the dish in America predates the use of this emigrant port by three decades or more. American restaurants of the earlier nineteenth century charged a huge mark-up for these meats because grinders were expensive and not available to everyone. But when the home meat grinder became available in the middle of the century, the price went down. When the Chicago meatpacking industry began its trade in beef in earnest in the 1880s, it began to replace salt pork in the hearts of many Americans.

People found early on that "catsup" went very well with this beef. A version adapted from the *American Frugal Housewife* by Lydia Child is "delicious with roast meat." It's important when making homemade catsup to free the mind of contemporary ketchup—Heinz and the like. This is more like tomato sauce than modern ketchup, whether spelled with a "c" or "k." It is chunky and should keep in the fridge for a week or more. If you are interested in bottling it for keeping and making it a little more recognizable for today's eaters, puree the result for smoothness, add significant sugar and vinegar and can or bottle it with proper sterilization:

Catsup
. . . .

6 large tomatoes

2 teaspoons kosher salt

1 cup water

½ cup apple cider

2 tablespoons sugar

¼–½ teaspoon each of cloves, allspice, mace

½ teaspoon black pepper

1 teaspoon garlic, minced

2 tablespoons vinegar

To remove skins, score the skins gently with a knife at the bottom and top of the tomato. This helps when peeling. Place the tomatoes in a large pot and slowly pour boiling water on them. Blanch for 20–30 seconds and then remove tomatoes to a bowl of cold water. Let stand a few minutes and then peel the skin. Quarter tomatoes and remove any bruises. Place a colander under a large bowl and "[squeeze them] up in the hand" separating as many seeds as possible. Put pulp and juice in the bowl. Sprinkle salt over the tomatoes and set in the fridge for a few hours or overnight. Press the pulp through a sieve, removing as much juice and as many seeds as possible. Dispose of juice—it's salty and affects the final product if used. Place the pulp in a medium saucepan; add fresh water and apple cider, sugar and spices (cloves are a little strong for modern tastes, so feel free to try different spices, like coriander).

Boil until reduced by half. Stir in vinegar and bottle when cool, storing in the fridge. The salt and spice will "keep the catsup well."

Finding the right accompaniment for ground beef was a step forward. However, the key was to make it portable. If a restaurant could sell this cheap and popular dish somehow to factory workers and other city dwellers at lunchtime, and allow them to carry it away, then they might have something tasty and quick.

The revolution happened sometime around the turn of the twentieth century. In the early 1900s, "Hamburger Charlie" from Wisconsin claimed to have invented the hamburger when he made it in the 1880s, even though his evidence only begins decades later. Later, a partisan writer quoted a *New York Tribune* article that doesn't exist to claim the burger's invention in Texas in 1905. A frequently mentioned Delmonico's menu item from the 1830s is a complete fake. So, by far the best and mostly carefully documented claim for the first restaurant to serve a ground meat patty between two pieces of bread is New Haven's Louis Lunch. The small lunch wagon opened in 1895 and seems to have never served anything else but these burgers. Their existence easily goes back to the opening of the permanent lunch location in 1900. The same vertical broilers exist, and the sworn affidavits are contemporary and hard to argue with.

Some purists argue that this is not a hamburger because it uses toast instead of a "bun," but if that is the case, then the first "hamburgers" were created by White Castle in 1916, and this is a questionable assertion in itself. It is a little like trying to figure out the inventor of a popular phrase. No doubt some street-food vendor put ground meat patties between bread even before Louis Lunch did it, just as someone said "a rose by any other name would smell as sweet" before Shakespeare. But Louis Lunch was the first documented eatery to do it and is certainly the only place to have lasted long enough to deserve the title. At the very least, it is the oldest-surviving hamburger joint in the nation.

What's even better is that this little restaurant still exists, and you can go there today. The original site was moved to George Street in 1906, and in 1975, it moved to Crown, but you can still see the decades of initials carved into the benches and counters of the tiny building. The surprisingly lean meat patties and onions (available on request) are put in antique, cast-iron vertical broilers, powered by gas. These fascinating machines of the steampunk age flame-broil the burgers evenly on both sides. When done, they are placed on Pepperidge Farm white toast.

There's only one caveat: don't ask for ketchup or mustard. The garnishes include cheese, tomato and onion, and there's really no point in putting tomato sugar or pungent mustard seed on the meat. That would only ruin it. The Louis Lunch burger with toast is a different experience; the meat stands out more, and there's nothing like the taste of tradition. As for trying to make these unique burgers at home, good luck. There is something about Louis' impossible-to-buy grills that is un-reproducible. This is due not only to the odd way the meat

Fire-grilled patties have been served at Louis Lunch since 1895, making it the oldest hamburger joint in the nation. *Courtesy of the authors.*

is cooked but also the fact that these particular broilers have been around since 1898. Like the brick ovens at Frank Pepe's Pizzeria Napoletana (see next chapter), the vertical toasters' molecular structures have changed in a way that transfers to and improves the food.

There are other hamburger trailblazers in Connecticut, like Harry's Place, making burgers since 1918 in Colchester. They keep a hot, oiled griddle and cook the burger in a large ellipse, squashing it down with a spatula just before placing it on your roll. This method keeps the burger juicy in a very different way than the famous steamed burgers that also seem to have been invented locally. Legendary road food experts Jane and Michael Stern noted this oddity in their travels around America and never found it anywhere else.

The origins remain uncertain, but steamed burgers may have been first made in Middletown in the 1920s or even earlier, possibly at a place called Jack's Lunch. At some

O'Rourke's Diner in Middletown is one of the best places to get a true Connecticut original: the steamed cheeseburger. *Courtesy of the authors.*

point, the style moved west into Meriden. In 1941, steamed burgers were brought back to Middletown by John O'Rourke, uncle of the current owner of O'Rourke's Diner. Then, in 1959, Ted's restaurant opened in Meriden as a family-operated business and has stayed that way, passing to Ted's son, Paul, who made changes like grinding the meat twice and using a sturdier cheddar. He also helped develop the steam box and trays that are used at area restaurants today. As the idea spread, small changes like the toasted buns at Higgie's in nearby Higganum were incorporated. The traditional toppings for the steamed cheeseburger in the mid-twentieth century were a little bit of mustard and onion. Today, people want it "their way"—and most restaurants comply.

At O'Rourke's Diner in Middletown today, over 50 percent of the customers are regulars—an astonishingly loyal fan base. One reason is the expansive, foodie menu. The other may be the care they put into this unique Connecticut invention. O'Rourke's uses fresh ground beef from a local purveyor and well-aged sharp cheddar cheese, which matches the beef better and melts properly. They also buy frozen dough and then proof and bake the hard rolls that day. The steamer is essentially a double broiler, mostly sealed, that contains shelves with holes. The chopped beef patties go onto the small plastic trays and slip inside. The cheese stays in the steamer all day in a separate metal tray. The burger has a very beefy flavor, rather than the charred taste of a grill. It gets very juicy, and the gooey melted cheese and fresh roll complement it perfectly.

While sampling these Connecticut originals in the diner is relatively easy, especially if you're located in the middle of the state, making steamed cheeseburgers at home necessitates some special equipment. You can buy your own plastic trays and steam cheeseburger "chest" from Burg'r Tend'r, easily found online. Commercial units run over $500 and have to be replaced if you let the water run out and burn the bottom—one reason these have not caught on nationwide. The small home units still cost almost $300, though those who have them swear by them. We'll assume you'd rather spend $30 for a Chinese three-tiered industrial aluminum steamer and use small bread or baking pans (we used 3x5 baking dishes):

Steamed Cheeseburgers

The oldest, sharpest cheddar you can find (about 6 ounces)
20 ounces ground beef
4 fresh-baked hard rolls
Seasoning to taste

In the bottom bin of the steamer, bring 2 cups of water to a boil. Grate cheese into a small metal bread pan and place the pan in one of the steamer tiers above the water. Cover and steam the cheese for about 20 minutes, stirring occasionally to break down the enzymes and fats for a smooth mixture. In the meantime, mix ground beef in a small bowl with any desired seasonings—Worcestershire sauce, pepper, etc. Form small patties, not too big, about 5 ounces each, and place in small pans.

After the cheese is significantly melted, remove the tier and replace it with the one holding the burgers. Place the cheese tier on top and steam both for 4–5 minutes, until burgers are done. Remove the burgers with a slotted spatula, being careful to dislodge excess grease. Keep the cheese tray steaming while plating the burgers, as it will start to harden if left out too long. Take care to use sturdy rolls, ones that will hold the juiciness of the burgers, like fresh brioche burger buns from Judie's European Bakery in New Haven. Top the plated burgers with melted cheese and serve. Eat immediately with ketchup if you like, or with roasted onions, but don't clutter the burger too much. Savor the essence of meat and enjoy its melted marriage with gooey cheese.

Doing this at home is not exactly "fast food" or a "quick lunch," but then again, firing up a charcoal grill takes a while, too. Restaurants like O'Rourke's or Louis Lunch can make hamburgers for us speedily because they do it in volume. Either we home cooks work for flavor or we submit to the worst impulses that Stephen Vincent Benet decried a century ago, resulting in food that can be barely called food. The hamburger is our heritage, and it deserves our close attention and care, as cooks and as diners, as citizens of Connecticut and as Americans.

1 6

New Haven Style

New Yorkers have the best claim to inventing pizza, and they are probably correct. However, Connecticut has produced something unique: a signature thin-crust pie baked in a super-hot brick oven and topped with tomato sauce and "mootz." The Italian immigrants who surged into the state in the late 1800s and early 1900s are responsible for this wonderful invention and for so many other culinary delights. The coincidence of this influx with the increased availability of global goods at this time made the impact of their contribution to our cuisine even greater. Olive oil, garlic and tomatoes seem so intertwined with our food today that it is hard to imagine life without them. And life without pizza? Well, that is best left unimagined.

Tomatoes were virtually unknown in the state until the 1830s, and only somewhat popular before the great influx of southern Europeans at the turn of the twentieth century, but they never grew well enough to become an export. Tomato sauce was certainly used to enhance a variety of different foods, from clams to chickens. Here's an old recipe for the sort of sauce they made in the nineteenth century:

Tomato Sauce

1 large onion, chopped
1 clove garlic, minced
½ cup olive oil
1 quart tomatoes, peeled,
    seeded and chopped
1 six-ounce can tomato paste

Salt and pepper
1 bay leaf
1 teaspoon basil
½ teaspoon thyme
½ teaspoon oregano

In a saucepan, sauté onion and garlic in olive oil until tender. Add tomatoes and paste and cook over medium-low heat for 1 hour. Add seasoning and cook for 5–10 minutes before serving or storing.

Frank Pepe's first bakery, where he invented the coal-fired thin-crust pizzas that define New Haven style. *Courtesy of Frank Pepe's Pizzeria Napoletana.*

Despite the inclusion of garlic in this recipe, before the Italians came to Connecticut, the philosophy was, as outlined by Lucy Emerson, "garlics are better adapted to the uses of medicine than cookery." These newcomers soon changed that opinion as the wonderful smell of these roasting cloves reached the noses of their neighbors.

Born in 1893 in a small Amalfi Coast village, Frank Pepe immigrated to New Haven at age sixteen, returning briefly to fight for Italy in World War I. After a stint in various bakeries and "macaroni" restaurants in town, he gathered the money to open a bakery at 163 Wooster Street. The Neapolitan "pizza" dish, only two decades old in America, was on the menu and quickly became a favorite.

Frank Pepe baked four or five pizzas, stacked them on his head and took them to the nearby market, selling them by the slice for ten cents or a whole pie for twenty-five. At first he just had "Alicia" (anchovy) and "plain," with only a little sprinkle of pecorino romano (and no mozzarella). Indeed, mozzarella remains a "topping" in southern Connecticut, and people from around the country who ask for "plain" pizza here, expecting it to mean "cheese," are in for a surprise. The dish is also called "apizza," pronounced "ah-beetz," a term now ubiquitous in the state.

In 1936, in a stroke of genius, he built the tile-encased coal-burning oven that bakes at 650 degrees. This gives the crust a scorched, caramelized *umami* that is matched by the chewy center. He used high-quality ingredients, including local clams, creating the "white clam pie" that is so famous today, complete with freshly shucked littleneck clams. The taste of clams is subtle and works well with olive oil, garlic, freshly grated cheese and the hint of coal.

Barely a block away from Pepe's, his nephew Sal and his wife, Flo Consiglio, opened their pizza restaurant in 1938, purchasing their iconic twelve- by twelve-foot brick oven four years later. It fits twenty pies, heats to seven hundred degrees and, like Pepe's, is coal-fired. "Sally's" simple menu only includes pizza: mozzarella, anchovy, bacon, sausage, tuna, onion, mushroom, peppers, plain, pepperoni, fresh tomato, hot cherry peppers, olives and, of course, clams. Sally's red sauce is sweeter and tarter than Pepe's, with less cheese overall, leading to a different balance in its pies. The pie is crisp from crust to center, and there are no tricks of herbs or additives.

To the uninitiated, the blackened crust on Sally's White Clam Pizza is a turnoff, but a true aficionado knows this signals authentic New Haven style. *Courtesy of the authors.*

The rivalry between these two restaurants divides a city, and a nation, with celebrities and critics taking sides, from John Kennedy to Ronald Reagan and Frank Sinatra to Robert DeNiro. Lines stretch down the block at both restaurants on any given night, and people brave the winter cold and hour-long waits to get a slice of these amazing pies. One reason they do is that making these pies yourself is nearly impossible, unless you have a coal-fired brick oven that goes up to seven hundred degrees, a baker's peel and a pizza stone. Even if you do, there is something un-reproducible, something that has changed in the molecular structure of an oven that has made millions of pies over decades, a seasoning beyond mere seasoning. But that doesn't mean you shouldn't try:

New Haven-Style White Clam Pizza

DOUGH

1 package dry active yeast

1 teaspoon sugar

1 cup warm water

1 teaspoon olive oil

1 teaspoon salt

3 cups flour, plus extra for kneading

Cornmeal

TOPPING

2 dozen little neck clams (1 cup chopped)

3 garlic cloves, finely chopped

1 teaspoon dried oregano or 1 tablespoon fresh

4 tablespoons olive oil

½ cup Italian pecorino romano cheese, grated

In a bowl, mix yeast and sugar until dissolved in water. Let stand a few minutes, then add, oil, salt and flour and mix with a sturdy wooden spoon or in a food processor. Turn the dough onto a floured surface and knead well until it becomes somewhat elastic, about 10 minutes. Add more flour if needed. Place dough in a bowl lightly coated with oil and turn the dough in the bowl until coated. Let it rise in a warm place until doubled in size, 30–60 minutes. Preheat oven (and pizza stone if you have one) to 500. Toss a little cornmeal onto a surface and shape dough into an 18-inch pie, or divide dough and shape it into two smaller pies. Dough should be thin—about ¼-inch thick and slightly thicker at the edges. Top with clams, chopped garlic, oregano, drizzled olive oil and sprinkled cheese. Bake on a pizza stone or baking sheets for about 15 minutes. While reproducing the coal fire effects is difficult to do, you want a super-hot oven to give the crust a little burn. Experiment with oregano; Pepe's style definitely includes it, while Sally's version lets the garlic and olive oil work alone. If you prefer, mozzarella can be substituted for pecorino romano, but don't use too much or the clams will get lost.

Italian immigrants to the state began to leave their mark on more than pizza. In 1926, Benedetto Capalbo brought the Italian sandwich to America at 18 Shaw Street in New London. During World War II, soldiers from the nearby submarine base ate them by the thousands. At the same time, the Nardelli brothers opened their grocery in Waterbury. They took the Italian sandwich and the New York "grinder" and made their own version, now a Connecticut classic. Here's Tony Nardelli's version:

Nardelli's Italian Combo Grinder

2 green bell peppers

1 cucumber

½ onion

1 cup store-bought Italian salad dressing

1 12-inch loaf Italian bread
    (about 1¼ pounds)

1½ cups iceberg lettuce, shredded

15 kalamata olives, pitted and sliced

Hot sauce

⅓ pound ham, thinly sliced

1 tomato, sliced

1 cubanelle pepper, seeded and thinly sliced

Banana peppers, sliced into rings

⅓ pound soppressata, thinly sliced

5 thin slices asiago cheese

⅓ pound capicola or prosciutto, sliced

In a large bowl, chop and combine the bell peppers, cucumber, onion and salad dressing. Let sit for 30 minutes or overnight. Drain, reserving the marinade. Halve the bread lengthwise and scoop out the top half. Drizzle both sides with the reserved marinade. Place the lettuce on the bread bottom and top with the olives and half of the marinated vegetables; season with the hot sauce. Top with the ham, tomato, cubanelle pepper, banana peppers, soppressata, asiago and capicola. Set the bread top in place and cut crosswise into 4 sandwiches. Serve with the remaining marinated vegetables.

The Nardelli family continues to operate a string of sandwich shops throughout central Connecticut. One of their culinary heirs is Fred DeLuca of Bridgeport. He opened Pete's Submarines in 1965 when he was only seventeen years old, changing the name to Pete's Subway and eventually Subway. This Connecticut-born sandwich shop now operates in nearly one hundred countries, with tens of thousands of franchises across the globe. And Subway is not the only one. The methods and innovations of Connecticut's Italian Americans have gone national and global. In fact, things like pizzas and grinders are no longer "Italian" cuisine but American cuisine itself.

Waiting in line outside a restaurant seemingly too small to be so legendary or sitting in the vinyl benches on a cold January evening, bracing against the cold when the door swings open and another group of hungry eaters comes in for a table, you find yourself momentarily experiencing the unimaginable—life without pizza—wondering if those around you can hear the grumble of your belly, unsure if the legend will hold up. Glance around at accolades and old photos, testaments to innovation, to tradition, to sharing the good life. Once the slice arrives, with a sip of cold beer or Foxon Park's cream soda, you are not sorry for waiting, only satisfied, proud that things as basic as dough and sauce, heat and time, none of which we have exclusive ownership of, can tell us our place in the world. Here you sit in Connecticut, sandwiched between past, present and future.

Happiness Is a Good Dog

Whether you call them hot dogs, frankfurters, wieners, sausages or brats, there is something about cased tube meat in a roll that has a hold on the American mind. And Connecticut knows how to do them right, with dozens of classic eateries and recipes across the landscape. *Serious Eats* calls Connecticut "a state that deserves a hot dog tour in itself." And there are many dog variations in Connecticut, without a single regional style like the red snappers of Maine or the half-smokes of our nation's capital. Many hot dog joints use local Hummel, Muck or Rosol sausages and in the past used the great Grote and Weigel dogs. Some are grilled and some boiled, while the rolls alternate between side-spilt and split-top. Restaurants and their patrons argue about these choices with real seriousness, and die-hard fans swear by certain hot dogs with seemingly spiritual fervor.

Why Connecticut became one of the great hot dog states seems a mystery at first, until you look at a history of our relationship with tubular meat. For the first few centuries of European occupation of Connecticut, everyone made sausage at home. At slaughter time in November, everyone got together to process the meat, which needed to be preserved in various ways for the winter. Sausages, rolliches and headcheese were always made. Meat was cut off the bone in half-inch pieces and put into a large wooden box, where it was then chopped into fine ground beef or pork.

Catharine Beecher tells us that to prepare sausages you should wash the casings, in her time made from the intestines of sheep, and cut them into two-yard lengths. "Take a candle rod, and fastening one end of a case to the top of it, turn the case inside outward." Then wash and scrape "with a scraper made for the purpose." Soak the transparent, thin casings in salt water until ready. For the meat, use a ratio of one-third fat to two-thirds lean, and for every twelve pounds add twelve "large even spoonfuls of pounded salt, nine of sifted sage, and six of sifted black pepper. Some like a little summer savory. Keep in a cool dry place."

In *New England Cookery*, Lucy Emerson says to take "six pounds of good pork, free from skin, gristles, and fat," cutting and beating it until fine. Then, finely shred an equal amount of skinless beef-suet and "spread your meat on a clean dresser or table, then shake the sage all over, about three large spoonfuls." Add and mix lemon rind, sweet herbs, two grated nutmegs, two teaspoonfuls of pepper and a tablespoon of salt. Then, "clean some guts and fill them." She suggests frying these sausages with apples.

This ad from the turn of the twentieth century shows that making sausage at home was no longer a common practice. *From* New Kirmesse Cookbook.

As immigrants from places like Italy and Poland settled in the state, they brought their recipes and methods along with them, seasoning and smoking the smooth casings of meat to perfection. A recipe for a "Connecticut Bean Pot" from the *New England Heritage Cookbook* draws on all those traditions, using sausage, kielbasa and franks to make a mostly meat delight. Slice a pound each of hot Italian sausage, sweet sausage and Polish kielbasa, as well as three onions, and cook these in a casserole dish on the stove. Add a half teaspoon thyme, a half teaspoon basil, two bay leaves, three-fourths cup dry sherry, an eight-ounce can of tomato sauce and two one-pound cans of pork and beans, bringing it to a boil before transferring to the oven at 350 degrees. Cook for an hour and a half, adding chopped frankfurters in the last twenty minutes.

However, what made the hot dog different from the centuries of sausage-making past was the bun. And here in the Northeast, we developed our own style of bun: a split-top with flat sides that make it easy to grill or toast. These are the buns that make lobster rolls possible, as well. And in fact, the very idea of side-cut buns seems strangely awkward after you get used to our version:

New England-Style Hot Dog Buns

1 teaspoon dry yeast

1 teaspoon sugar

1 teaspoon salt

4 cups flour

½ cup milk

4 tablespoons unsalted butter

3 large eggs

½ cup water

2 tablespoons salad oil

126

Combine yeast and sugar with ¼ cup warm water in a bowl and let it stand for 10 minutes, until frothy. Add salt, flour, milk, 3 tablespoons melted butter and 2 beaten eggs. Mix while adding water. Knead dough for 5 minutes or more until soft and dense. Shape into a ball and place in a lightly oiled bowl. Let it rise in a warm place under a towel for 1 hour. Punch the dough, dusting the counter with flour. Shape it into a square, cutting it into 13 equal cylindrical pieces of 7 inches with a knife. Grease a baking sheet and put the pieces side by side on the sheet, leaving ½ inch between them. Let them rise. Using the last egg and 2 tablespoons water, make an egg wash and brush onto the dough. Continue to let it rise another 10 minutes or so while you preheat the oven to 350 degrees. Cook buns for about 30 minutes until golden brown and then let them cool on the sheet for about 15 minutes. Carefully remove them with a spatula and place on a rack to cool further. Then, top-cut them to load in the meat. Eaten fresh, these buns are soft and chewy; buttered and grilled or toasted, they are a completely different experience, beloved by many.

With the rise of urban populations in the twentieth century, hot dogs became more and more the province of large producers. They were sold to stores and fast-food joints, which in turn sold them to the consumer. Connecticut quickly became a leader in production and experimentation with methods and presentation. In 1925, at Savin Rock Amusement Park, the split hot dog was invented, supposedly when a customer saw his trolley car coming and urged the grill man to "hurry it up." Splitting the hot dog in half grilled it faster and in fact coated more of it with savory, caramelized char. Rawley's Drive-In in Fairfield, frequented by celebrities, took this split dog method in 1946 and went a little further. Using Roessler's beef-and-pork dogs, Rawley's deep-fries them in hot oil and then throws them on a griddle to drain off the oil and further blister the meat. They are stuffed into buttered, toasted rolls and often topped with crumbled bacon and sauerkraut. It is difficult to imagine a crispier, snappier hot dog.

However, condiments are where Connecticut hot dogs truly shine. In 1928, Art Blackman opened his hot dog stand in Cheshire, and it quickly became legend. Traditions like "no French fries," birch beer on tap and closing on Fridays per Catholic tradition have been kept since then. "No Dancing" signs were posted to avoid the Cabaret Tax and remain there today. But the most famous tradition is the secret family recipe for a hot pepper relish that remains a mystery. The following recipe is as close as we can come to the secret relish. Feel free to get some jars at Blackie's, compare and experiment:

Almost Blackie's Hot Dog Relish

5 green peppers, seeds removed

5 red peppers

5–10 hot peppers

5 onions

½ cup brown sugar

1½ tablespoons salt

½ teaspoon cinnamon

2 teaspoons allspice

¼ teaspoon nutmeg

2 cups cider vinegar

Remove the seeds from the green and red peppers but not the hot peppers. Use a food processor and grind up peppers and chopped onions. Put everything in a pot and simmer for 1½ hours or so and then pack in jars to chill. Take out as needed to spread on your dogs.

Cited as one of the top ten hot dog joints in America, Frankie's in Waterbury, opened in 1937 by the Caiazzo brothers, also has an amazing relish. Their sign, "The secret of happiness is a good dog," could be a motto for the entire state. But many other Connecticut restaurants serve meat sauces with their dogs, and each has its own wonderful variation. Opened in 1967 in Southington, Saint's has "chili dogs" with mustard, relish and a sweet, not very meaty sauce. Capitol Lunch in New Britain has a secret brown sauce on its "Cappie Dogs," with meat, a hint of clove and savory tomato sauce. And although it no longer exists, Tommie's Restaurant in Hartford had one of these great meat-based sauces, created by Greek immigrant "Tommie" and kept a secret. However, Lorraine French of Bristol re-created this amazing sauce for the *Hog River Journal* a few years ago, and her version is delicious:

Tommie-Style Meat Sauce

1 pound hamburger	1½ teaspoons cayenne pepper
1 onion, chopped fine	1½ teaspoons salt
2 cloves garlic, minced	1½ teaspoons pepper
1 tablespoon oil	2 teaspoons cumin
¼ teaspoon cloves	1 tablespoon paprika
¼ teaspoon cinnamon	1 tablespoon Worcestershire sauce
½ teaspoon oregano	2 tablespoons chili powder
1 teaspoon sugar	2 tablespoons tomato paste or ketchup
1 teaspoon allspice	

Fry meat, onion and garlic in oil for about 10 minutes, adding seasonings; keep chopping at the mixture to break it up. Add other ingredients and water. Simmer for 30–60 minutes. To thicken, add bread crumbs. Adjust seasonings to taste.

Connecticut cooks and chefs continue to push the envelope of hot dog cuisine. Culinary Institute of America grad Gary Zemola's restaurant Super Duper Weenie in Fairfield has only been around since 1992 but has won immediate fame with freshly baked bread, a selection of relishes made from homemade pickled vegetables and barrel-style sauerkraut spiked with toasted caraway and bacon. The "New Englander" dog includes sauerkraut, onion, bacon, mustard and relish. And other pioneers continue to forge ahead. Kenneth Giannetta and Joe Hamel of Two Guys One Grill in Wallingford have taken the hot dog concept and created a "chicken dog." But it does not use a chicken sausage; instead, it uses a piece of fried chicken in

The Waterbury institution of Frankie's still draws huge crowds today with its amusing but truthful motto, "Come in and eat or we'll both starve." *Courtesy of the authors.*

a top-loading New England hot dog roll, garnished with a selection of delicious sauces. This innovation makes complete sense, and it won't be long before it is popularized throughout the state and perhaps the country:

Two Guys Chicken Dogs

2 pounds chicken breast, boned

1 cup flour

2 eggs

1 package seasoned bread crumbs

1 package hot dog buns

Cut chicken breast into strips lengthwise. Lightly dredge strips into the flour, leaving a nice even coating. Then soak the flour-covered strips in the beaten eggs until they are covered entirely. Roll the flour/egg-covered strips in the seasoned bread crumbs until fully breaded. Finally, heat a shallow amount of oil in a large frying pan on medium-high. When oil is hot, place the breaded chicken strips in the oil, cooking evenly on both sides until golden brown and the meat is white and tender. Meanwhile, lightly toast the hot dog buns and prepare your favorite buffalo or barbecue sauce. Two Guys One Grill offers a variety of toppings, including a buffalo sauce made from cooking hot sauce, butter and sugar together, and MTS sauce, a mix of barbecue sauce and extra-thick mayonnaise. The buffalo and blue cheese chicken dog is a revelation—a familiar taste in a new setting.

As Two Guys One Grill and these other Connecticut establishments show us, the meat may be center stage, but the toppings and the buns make these local classics, rated on various "best" lists in magazines, newspapers and public opinion. Which is really the best? You'll have to try them all and let your stomach decide. But perhaps, instead of spending so much time arguing about the top dog, the greatest tribute we home chefs can offer is to try to replicate their works of genius ourselves.

PART VI

The Sweetest State:
Pudding, Pastry and Candy

From Holy Pokes
to Grape-Nuts Pudding

One of the first things visitors notice about Connecticut is the unusual number of doughnut shops. In fact, people rarely seem to eat anything else for breakfast, and the drive-through lines at local and chain shops stretch around blocks at all times of day. A town of fifty thousand people may have as many as ten doughnut shops—a staggering figure in most other areas of the country. But this should not be surprising. In a region where "puddings" and "pies" were considered proper meals for centuries, eating fried cakes for breakfast is no new development. The production of tasty desserts that were consumed as leftovers the following morning was one of the first culinary traditions in New England, and these puddings, pies, cakes and doughnuts continue to delight.

Sweet rolls for breakfast with coffee or tea first came into fashion at the end of the 1600s and never went out. In her father's *Autobiography*, a letter from Catharine Beecher mentions that on the occasion of the "wood-spell," when parishioners would bring the pastor sled loads of wood, "doughnuts and loaf-cake, cider and flip" were served. She writes:

> *For preliminaries, the fat was to be prepared to boil the dough-nuts, the spices to be pounded, the sugar to be rolled, the flour to be sifted, and the materials for beer for the flip to be collected. Next came the brewing, on a scale of grandeur befitting the occasion. Then the cake was fully made, and placed on large stone pots or earthen jars set around the kitchen fire and duly turned and tended till the proper lightness was detected. Lastly came the baking of the loaves and the boiling of the dough-nuts; and were I to tell the number of loaves I put into and took out of the oven, and the bushels of dough-nuts I boiled over the kitchen fire, I fear my credit for veracity would be endangered.*

Early recipes for doughnuts include "holy pokes," made with thin pieces of set bread dough, dropped into hot fat and browned on both sides. They were served with hot butter and maple syrup. "Crullers" were made with five cups flour, one cup butter, two cups sugar, a spoonful of rosewater and nutmeg. Putney resident Mary Etta Beach's recipe for crullers used milk and eggs rather than butter.

The main difference among doughnut recipes seems whether to use eggs or not. The old English recipe that many followed instructed, "To one pound of flour, put one quarter of a pound of butter, one quarter of a pound of sugar, and two spoonfuls of yeast; mix them all together in warm milk or water, or the thickness of bread, let it raise, and make them in what form you please, boil your fat (consisting of hog's lard), and put them in." However, both recipes by Catharine Beecher in the 1800s used eggs, though one called Walnut Hill Doughnuts also used sour cream. Mace, cinnamon or nutmeg are the most common flavorings. Beecher suggested "diamond-shaped" pieces for doughnuts rather than our current "torus" shape. But all agree that the key is frying in lard, hot enough so the cake will not absorb the fat:

Doughnuts

1 cup milk
½ cup butter
4 cups flour
½ teaspoon salt
½ cup sugar
1 package dry active yeast
Fat or oil

Heat milk until it begins to bubble at the edges. Add butter and melt it away from the burner, letting it cool slightly. Combine dry ingredients in a separate bowl and then add milk and mix to form a batter. Cover and let rise in a warm place until doubled. Form dough into small balls, about a teaspoon, or roll out and form into circles. Alternatively, roll out thick and cut with circular cutters, to form the doughnut shape. Drop into heated oil (or lard if you can get it). When they rise to the top and are browned, remove with a slotted spoon and drain on paper towels. Dust with sugar, cinnamon, nutmeg or confectioner's sugar.

These circles of powdered, glazed or filled doughy goodness clearly hold a special place in our hearts. But they are not the only dessert-breakfast we enjoy. Pies have always been a popular dessert also served for breakfast, and although fruit was the most frequently added filling, cooks put in whatever else tasted good, especially nuts.

The Frisbie Pie Company was probably the first in the world to mass produce pies, but we remember them for their aerodynamic tin plates. *Courtesy of the Bridgeport History Center.*

One interesting variation used water chinquapin nuts, the seeds of the American lotus lily, found in shallow bays along the Connecticut coast. The Native Americans showed the colonists that these were edible, and the colonists, of course, put them in pies. To make a nut pie, with or without chinquapins, you would pour a half cup of boiling water over a cup of raisins and then let them cool to absorb. Then you would stir one cup of sugar into one cup of sour cream, break in an egg and beat until fluffy. Adding a half cup of nuts, a pinch of salt and a dash of vanilla and lemon, you would pour the entire mixture into a crust and bake it, covering it later with meringue, creating a rich and nutty pie.

Rum was also used in the kitchen as an important addition to cooking and baking, either as a flavor enhancer or as a headliner. In recipes like this one for rum pie, adapted from the *Mark Twain Library Cookbook*, it becomes the principal characteristic:

Rum Pie

. . . .

GRAHAM CRACKER CRUST

½ cup melted butter

2 cups graham cracker crumbs

¼ cup sugar

Combine ingredients in a bowl. Press mixture into a 9-inch pie plate. Cook in a 400-degree oven for 10 minutes. Cool in the fridge until filling is ready.

FILLING

1½ cups milk

¾ cup sugar

Pinch of salt

5 egg yolks

¼ cup flour

2 tablespoons cornstarch

½ stick butter, softened

3 tablespoons dark rum

In a double boiler, heat milk, sugar and salt. In a separate bowl, beat egg yolks, milk, flour and cornstarch. Stir milk into egg mixture and cook. Stir occasionally and cook without letting it boil until thick and smooth. Remove from heat and cool slightly. Beat in butter and rum. Pour filling into crust and chill in the refrigerator. Serve with whipped cream and nutmeg if desired. The beautiful yellow color of this pie and the sweet hints of rum make it a tasty hit with all but the most committed teetotalers among us.

But perhaps the quintessential dessert for breakfast in Connecticut history is the pudding. Originally, it was made in "pudding bags," a technique we have lost in the modern kitchen. The most basic of these were flour or batter puddings, with fresh eggs, milk, salt and flour boiled in the pudding bag for almost an hour. Amelia Simmons added nutmeg and cinnamon to the basic combination, which varied widely in the number of eggs and the amount of sugar used. One recipe used two cups milk, six tablespoons flour, four eggs and a half teaspoon of salt. You would beat yolks thoroughly, stir in the flour and add milk slowly. Beat the whites of the eggs to froth and add them last, before tying in a floured bag and putting in boiling water for about two hours, allowing room for the mix to swell.

Simmons also suggested a Cream Almond Pudding, made by flavoring a quart of cream with mace and nutmeg and boiling. After cooling, you would mix in eight egg yolks, three egg whites, a spoon of flour, a quarter pound of almonds and a spoon of rosewater and cold cream "by degrees," then beat. "Wet a thick cloth and flour it, and pour in the pudding, boil hard for half an hour, take out and pour over it melted butter and sugar," she says, assured that every cook of the eighteenth century knew how to work one of these makeshift bags.

Most cooks mixed in fresh berries to these basic puddings. They could also be made with apples, pears, plums or even potatoes. Carrots, squash and pumpkin puddings were certainly meals rather than desserts, although cinnamon, nutmeg and sugar made them fairly sweet, like candied sweet potatoes or carrots would be today. A rennet (head) pudding is suggested "if your husband brings home company when you are unprepared," because it could be made quickly, as long as you had "a piece of calf's rennet ready." Soaking this in a mixture of wine and milk would make "a sort of cold custard," which could be sweetened, spiced and eaten immediately before curdling. Almost all of the variations of pudding used rosewater for flavoring. If imported oranges or lemons were available, the grated peel would be added to the basic recipe for flavoring, and this was enjoyed so much that these versions survived the great custard shift of the nineteenth century.

Today, custard usually uses eggs, and pudding usually does not. Like the rennet pudding, which needed no boiling, the cooks of the late eighteenth century began to make what we would consider baked custard rather than boiled pudding. The shift happened over a long time, and the words "pudding" and "custard" were used interchangeably throughout. Both could refer to dishes with or without eggs. One of the reasons for this shift seems to have been the improvements in ovens. In 1800, James Lamb of Middletown contributed to these improvements when he invented the Lamb cooking stove, not designed to cook lamb but rather the first to evenly distribute heat around the oven. Before these improvements, boiling in a bag was a way to ensure even cooking.

Interesting custard variations included rice custard and sickbed custard, which would be baked "on coals in a pewter vessel." In Simmons's time, they were typically made with milk or sweet cream, sweetened and heated, with eggs and spice added, and of course boiled or baked depending on preference. Rice custard would be flavored with mace, nutmeg and rosewater and was often served in cups rather than bowls. "Rich" custard used an equal number of eggs and cups of cream. An old Groton recipe for "pudding" included custard with cranberries and was served with a hot sauce made by melting butter in a double boiler and adding sugar and an alcoholic beverage of choice. Once well mixed, it was poured hot over the pudding.

Other sauces for puddings or custards included wine sauce, orange sauce, molasses sauce and maple syrup folded into cream and whipped stiff. A "healthful one" was made by boiling citrus peel or peach leaves in two cups of water and then mixing two tablespoons of flour with a little water to form a thickening agent. After boiling for five minutes, add a pint of brown sugar and boil again. Add two tablespoons of butter and a glass of wine and then remove from the heat just before it boils. Their definition of "healthful" was clearly slightly different from ours.

In the twentieth century, the introduction of Post cereal's Grape-Nuts led to an interesting twist on the old custards and puddings. Grape-Nuts Pudding seems like a strange invention, but it works so well, it's hard to believe the cereal was not invented for this purpose. The cereal is actually malted bread crumbs: shredded, dried and crushed wheat-and-barley bread. These small, knobbly "grape nuts" form a delicious savory layer on top or on the bottom of the sweet yellow custard, depending on the recipe and the chef. The adaptation below is a combination of several recipes and makes sweet custard that does not need one of the sauces listed above or even whipped cream:

Grape-Nuts Pudding

4 eggs
1 cup sugar
1½ cups skim milk
½ cup light cream

1 teaspoon vanilla
½ teaspoon cinnamon
¼ teaspoon freshly grated nutmeg
½ cup Grape-Nuts cereal, plus ¼ cup

Mix eggs, sugar, milk, cream, vanilla, cinnamon and nutmeg. Pour into an 11- x 7-inch baking dish. Sprinkle ½ cup Grape-Nuts over the top. Place pudding in a larger pan (10.5 x 14.75 inches) and slowly pour hot water around it to create a bath. Bake in an oven preheated to 350 degrees for 15 minutes. Sprinkle the additional Grape-Nuts over the top when the pudding is partially set. Bake for an additional 15 minutes. Turn off the oven and let the pudding begin to cool and further set. Remove after 5 or 10 minutes and serve warm.

Whether baked, boiled or fried, all these delightful mixtures of sugar, flour, milk and eggs make great desserts or breakfasts for the same reason: they are comfort foods that assuage or prevent the hungers of the day. What's more, these substantial indulgences have made our state the happy place it is for centuries. So, the next time you eat a doughnut at a local bakery or Grape-Nuts Pudding at a local diner, think kindly of all those full bellies before you and all those to come. And as Connecticut food and culture maven Martha Stewart might say, indulgence can be a good thing, whether at the beginning of a busy day or at its weary end.

Connecticut Confections

When the first thaw freed the tree sap, you harvested it through bored holes in maple trunks into wooden buckets, bringing the fluid in tanks on horse-drawn sleds to the sugarhouse. This began the oldest agricultural endeavor in the United States, boiling, concentrating and filtering the sap into bubbling maple syrup. The real fun was carrying some amber syrup outside and pouring it into the clean fresh snow, making swirling designs. Then, you grabbed and gobbled the glassy, taffy-like, sweet snow candy that was the delight of the year.

Some would say that it is difficult to improve on this frozen slab of sugar. But for centuries, sweet-toothed Connecticut innovators have been trying to do just that, using the ingredients of honey, molasses, chocolate and, of course, maple sugar. This sugar was produced in large quantities in hill towns like Goshen and Norfolk and was poured on pretty much everything from Indian pudding to slices of bread. It was also turned into maple sugar candy, whether crystallized instantly on the snow or boiling it in a three-to-two ratio with cream for about half an hour, stirring all the time. "When it stiffens in cold water, it is done"; then you could stir in nuts for a crunchier treat. But one of the most interesting ways it was eaten was in a "maple parfait," as in this recipe from Alice Johnson, director of the Friendly League School of Housekeeping one hundred years ago:

Maple Parfait

1 cup maple syrup
Yolks of 4 eggs
1 pint cream

Heat the syrup until it "begins to spin a thread" when a fork pulls it out. Then add the yolks, stirring and allowing to cool. Whip the cream stiff and then fold it into the cooled mixture. Put into the freezer and serve with whipped cream.

Wild honey was gathered from hollow tree trunks by early colonists, and later families kept hives near the farm for both honey for sweetener and wax for candles. Bees were raised for honey in Wethersfield already in 1648. Honey was a flavorful complement or primary confectionery ingredient, like in a one-hundred-year-old recipe for honey cookies that includes one-half cup butter, one-half cup sugar, one cup honey, two egg yolks, one-fourth teaspoon cinnamon, one teaspoon vanilla, three cups flour, three teaspoons baking powder, one-fourth cup chopped almonds, one-fourth cup citron and salt. After mixing, bake spoonful-sized rounds in a 350-degree oven for ten to fifteen minutes.

However, probably the most widely used sweetener from the late 1600s to the late 1800s was an import: molasses. Its reputation declined in the late 1800s as refined sugar became cheaper. But even as it did, molasses solidified in popular imagination as the necessary ingredient for gingerbread and gingerbread cookies, which developed into gingersnaps.

Everyone had her own gingersnaps recipe, though all proceeded from the simple ingredients of molasses and ginger. Catharine Beecher added sugar and butter, along with pearl ash for leavening. Nellie Coe of Stratford used lard. The following gingersnaps recipe is modified from the curiously long-titled 1836 book *New England Cook Book or Young Housekeeper's Guide: Being a Collection of the Most Valuable Receipts Embracing all the Various Branches of Cookery and Written in a Minute and Methodical Manner*:

Gingersnaps

....

¼ cup butter melted	*2 teaspoons powdered ginger*
¾ cup sugar	*1 teaspoon fresh minced fresh ginger with juice*
¾ cup molasses	*¼ teaspoon mace*
1 teaspoon baking soda	*¼ teaspoon allspice*
1 teaspoon cinnamon	*1½ cups flour*

Preheat oven to 325. Combine ingredients. If necessary, add more flour to form manageable dough. Roll out thin between parchment papers. Cut into circles, using a narrow glass (we used a sherry glass) dipped in sugar. Sprinkle lightly with sugar and place on a cooking sheet. Bake 8–10 minutes or until done. These are perfectly crunchy on the outside and chewy in the middle.

Along with molasses, sugar cane was imported. One cone of sugar, weighing ten or fifteen pounds, would sweeten a family for a year, cut into lumps with sugar shears. This sugar would be used to make various desserts and became popular for cookies, since unlike molasses, honey or maple sugar, it didn't add extra flavor to the mixture, just sweetness. Catharine Beecher gives a number of recipes for treats such as "New Year's Cookies," with sugar, butter, buttermilk, eggs, nutmeg and caraway seeds; Lemon Drop Cakes, with sifted white sugar, flour, lemon rinds and egg whites; and Sugar Drops, with twelve spoonfuls of butter, twenty-four spoonfuls of sifted white sugar, a pint of sifted flour, three eggs beaten separately and half a nutmeg. Plain cookies were made by boiling one pound of sugar slowly in a half pint of water, adding two teaspoons of pearl ash dissolved in milk and then adding two and a half pounds of flour and four ounces of butter, along with two tablespoons of coriander. These were baked for fifteen or twenty minutes in a "slack" oven. Spices like coriander and caraway and flavorings like lemon were subtle additions and gave the simplest cookie a little boost.

Sugar was also used in preservation, like when candying extra fruits and nuts. Candied ginger, lemon and orange peels were called suckets. Caraway seed confits and sweet meat jellies were also special treats. "Hard sauce" was made with confectioners' sugar, butter, brandy and sometimes cream and could be poured on anything needing a little sweetness. As improving technology coincided with the

Armenian immigrant Peter Paul Halajian began making candy at home, selling it to commuters at train stations in the Naugatuck Valley in the 1880s. *Courtesy of the Hamden Historical Society.*

Peter Paul's MOUNDS

What a bar of candy for 5¢!

...Tree-ripened coconut...delicious chocolate...One bite and you, too will say, "What a bar of candy for 5 cents!"

Peter Paul, Inc., Naugatuck, Conn.

wide availability of cane sugar, an entire candy industry sprang up in the state. In 1908, Bradley and Smith Company in New Haven first used a confectionery machine to make lollipops, named for a popular racehorse of the day, or an old form of softer candy, depending on the source. In 1973, Pez Candy's small pellets of flavored sugar began to be churned out of Orange. With their fruity flavors and dispensers featuring popular cartoon characters and celebrities of the day, these little candies have sold consistently and well, with three billion in the United States alone each year, without advertising.

Connecticut has also led the way in America's favorite sweet—chocolate—since Christopher Leffingwell of Norwich founded the first chocolate mill in America in 1770. During World War I, American soldiers developed a hunger for the Hershey chocolate bars they received in their rations. When they returned, candy bar manufacturers sprang up across the nation. One of these was founded by Armenian immigrant Peter Paul Halajian in 1919 in New Haven. A year later, he invented the Mounds bar, which became instantly popular. Its combination of coconut and dark chocolate was delicious and distinguished it from the other bars flooding the market. Peter Paul had to buy a larger factory to meet demand and purchased one in Naugatuck that was in operation for eighty-eight years. In the meantime, the Peter Paul Company added Almond Joy and York Peppermint Patties to the line, and they remain some of the most popular candy bars in America.

Peter Paul inspired a legion of Connecticut chocolatiers. Munson's Chocolates was founded by Ben and Josephine Munson in 1946, when it was called the Dandy Candy Company. First located in Manchester behind a tailor shop, the Munsons made wafers and ribbon candy from the sugar rations they received following the end of World War II. After moving to a converted horse barn and opening their first of many retail stores, they became hugely popular throughout the state and beyond, while remaining a family business.

Their pecan turtles are a tradition going back to 1946. The turtle recipe is top secret, like all their formulas, but you can start with the following and try to improve it. Take sixteen ounces of caramels and melt them in a very small amount of water, stirring. Then arrange about three-quarters of a pound of pecan halves on a cookie sheet, with each of these "naked" turtles about two inches apart. Take a teaspoon of caramel and dollop it onto the nuts. Allow it to cool. Meanwhile, melt a six-ounce package of semi-sweet chocolate chips and paint the chocolate on top of the caramel. Of course, Munson's uses very high-quality chocolate and caramel to make theirs, so by all means experiment beyond the packaged stuff in the grocery store.

Though not quite Switzerland, Connecticut is chock-full of gourmet chocolate producers, from Bridgewater in Brookfield to Belgique in Kent, from Knipshildt in Norwalk to Tschudin in Middletown. A standout is Fascia's Chocolates in Waterbury, begun in 1964. John and Helen Fascia began creating candy confections in their home, eventually creating a full-time family business that kept growing throughout the decades of the late twentieth century until today. Their truffles are particularly delightful. Here is their recipe:

Chocolatier Josephine Munson displays a mold from legendary candy manufacturer Stollwerck, which had a factory in Connecticut in the early twentieth century. *Courtesy of Munson's Chocolates.*

Ganache (Truffle Center)

1 cup heavy cream
2 tablespoons granulated sugar
4 tablespoons sweet butter
1 pound Fascia's dark chocolate
1 tablespoon flavor

Place heavy cream, sugar and butter in a microwave-safe bowl and heat on high for 2 minutes. Butter should melt, and cream should be hot but not boiling. Meanwhile, chop the chocolate into small pieces and place in a bowl. Pour the hot cream mixture over the chocolate pieces and stir gently until melted and smooth. If desired, add flavoring. Natural extract oils compatible with chocolate work best. Put in refrigerator to cool until the texture is pliable. Different flavorings will change the length of time for the center to set up into a rollable texture. Roll into balls using cocoa powder to help keep them from sticking. The ganache center can be coated with toppings such as coconut flakes or nuts and used as a finished product. For a true finished gourmet truffle, dip the center into properly tempered milk or dark chocolate. Shelf life is approximately 2–3 weeks refrigerated.

From maple sugar to Mounds bars, sweets have been more than just dessert; they are part of the state's identity. As Harriet Beecher Stowe wrote long ago, "I have a word to say under the head of Confectionery, meaning by this the whole range of ornamental cookery—or pastry, ices, jellies, preserves, etc. The art of making all these very perfectly is far better understood in America than the art of common cooking." Ironically, in a bout of provincial stuffiness this Connecticut author and epicure once declared the products of cocoa beans "unfit" for the table. Perhaps she would have changed her mind if she tried a Connecticut chocolate truffle.

Epilogue

Thanksgiving

Paging through a cookbook or pulling out three-by-five cards from grandmother's recipe box, we find individual treasures. The instructions tell us to synthesize—a little of this, a pinch of that, a hearty spoonful of the other. Mix and serve.

"Receipts," as they were once called, are vouchers of goodness, acknowledgement of traditions passed by mouth, passed by demonstration, mother to daughter, chef to chef, generation to generation. The unspoken becomes permanent, proof of the past, hope for another good, worthy meal. Every family collected them, scribbled on paper, transcribed and translated from every language. The family cookbook gathers the voices of the house, blends old and new, combines the nostalgia we hold for food with the desire to open the book of possibility.

Recipes are important, but one recipe and the dish it produces are only part of the picture. There's only one helping, until we color the plate and add another portion, make another dish, find another flavor. Until we have a meal. But there is even more. As our own Jacques Pepin says, "Food is an expression of love, because you always cook for 'the other'—wife, child, lovers, friends. Food is life." The meal is meant to be shared.

While the word "feast" has lost some of its cachet in modern English, in times when a plentiful bounty was not always a given, gathering to share a meal was both practical and hospitable. It's one of the great things we can do as social animals: gather together friends, family and strangers to celebrate plenty. Guests who stayed overnight were usually expected to help with the morning chores like milking cows or chopping wood. But they would be rewarded again with a breakfast meal that might have included fresh cream poured over berries or hasty pudding. Red flannel hash, invented from last night's leftovers, might accompany toast with tomatoes.

The traditional celebration of Thanksgiving began in colonial times and remains an essential part of our culture. *Courtesy of Hamden Historical Society.*

Mornings, afternoons, evenings—all were a chance to open the recipe book, create a menu, set the table and bring together people and food. Mealtime gatherings were important, reflected in the often-extravagant preparations. Writing in *Connecticut Magazine* in 1900, Louise Bunch recommends a late lunch of oyster cocktail, soup, mushrooms on toast, celery, cranberry sauce, salted almonds, roast turkey, giblet gravy, browned mashed potatoes, boiled onions, lettuce salad, crackers, wine jelly and macaroons. A midday meal was often the biggest of the day, a break from the labors on either side of eating. Tea parties or afternoon soirées were a much less formal affair than in England or the South. A sense of frolicsome democracy presided, with all the food piled on a central table that people nibbled from as they talked and gossiped.

These company gatherings seasoned the menus as much as any garnish. On more formal occasions, dinner became a true feast. A dinner party held at Mark Twain's home on May 11, 1887, included an orchestra of delectable dishes. The menu recorded in Mrs. Holcombe's diary featured clams on the half shell, clear soup with sherry, tomato aspic and lettuce with mayonnaise. Soft-shell crabs made an appearance with dressed cucumber, along with shad roe balls with cream shad sauce and asparagus with cream sauce on toast. For a main course, roast lamb appeared smothered with cream curry sauce and peas. Creamed sweetbreads and broiled squab on toast with Parisian potatoes rounded out the chief offerings. Roman punch, no doubt waiting on the sideboard in a crystal bowl, filled glasses. When dessert was served, guests could choose from ice cream in the shape of flowers, strawberries in cream, candies and bonbons. For those already too full to indulge, coffee would finish the meal.

The flavors and textures captured on the Twain family menu borrow from earth and sea, Old World and New. These synthesized elements cry out for a gathering of people. However, the constraints of everyday life and the cost of preparing such lavishness did and still does relegate such festivals to a few times a year—and so holidays become our "excuse" for pulling out the good dishware and putting on a show.

At the Hill-Stead Museum in Farmington, curators re-create architect Theodate Polk's Christmas to give us an idea of what might have been served: oysters, Yorkshire pudding and roast beef; dessert plum pudding and sweets. Afterward, men would share cigars and coffee in the dining room, while women retired to the parlor for coffee and cigarettes. In Hartford, we can still experience Christmas on Main Street at the house that belonged, since 1792, to Daniel and Sarah Butler. Their daughter married Reverend John James McCook in 1866, and diaries from Reverend McCook describe Christmases at the homestead. Dinner after church was in the formal dining room, decorated with garlands of holly. The menu included "mock turtle soup, roast turkey, cranberry pudding, mince and pumpkin pie, frozen pudding, nuts, fruits, biscuits and homemade jams and cider."

Perhaps the most visible feast that we have is Thanksgiving, which had been a New England tradition long before Abraham Lincoln made it a national holiday. In the 1700s, the late autumn date began to coalesce, and in the 1770s a Thursday in late November or early December became a tradition. A roast turkey was common, along with pumpkin pie. However, these meals often included chicken pie, ham, goose, roast beef, mutton, mincemeat pie, pickles, preserves, cranberry or currant pie, apple pie and a variety of puddings, all washed down with a healthy quantity of cider. Well-off families would add treats like chocolate, box raisins, Jamaican rum and gin.

At the time of the Revolution, the Olmsted family gathered in their two-story mansion a half mile from the Connecticut River. For a week leading up to the holiday, the children "had been pounding cinnamon and cloves in a gigantic lignum-vitae mortar, and chopping suet and meat for mince pies, and stoning raisins and slicing citron, and making the rafters of the old colonial homestead echo with the busy preparation for that apostle of festivals." Prepared spices would not arrive until the mid-1800s, and so the seasoning, such as pounded rock salt, had to be "made fresh." That might not seem too difficult, but the Olmsteds were preparing for four generations to arrive, nearly fifty people. That's a lot of turkeys and peppery chicken pies to make—and to eat. Jugs and pitchers of cider soon emptied, washing down steaming potatoes and turnips. No doubt those who helped prepare the dinner were drawing upon handwritten recipes, tossing in a few inspired alterations and creating new memories with traditional fare.

These descriptions entice us with their savory detail and pull us into our own holiday memories. As the plate piles higher and higher, we should also remember that the feast of Thanksgiving celebrates the coming together of cultures, a time when hands were extended in welcome and help accepted, when the neighborhood was established. In the myth of Thanksgiving, we celebrate the survival from one harsh winter and a reminder that those winters, the arid summers and the flooded springs may come again. We give thanks for tradition, but we also save a spot at the table for the new. We learn, along the way, to relish the excitement of making a dish "to your taste," to discover for ourselves the beauty of substitutions, modifications and amendments. At the feast, we gather to appreciate new philosophies, new faces, new flavors—the panorama and the possibilities of our evolving nation.

At the Connecticut table, we gather and gaze out the window at diverse landscapes: the coastal water and its many creatures that tempt our tastes, the farms that show the way toward the harvest's bounty, old train tracks heading to city centers, where chefs make us dinner. We celebrate our shared heritage, whether our families came here long ago or we are just passing through, no matter how long we plan to stay. Our Connecticut cornucopia includes old favorites like Indian pudding and clam chowder; new entrants like chicken *arepas* and *kanibaba*; and those dishes we don't mark by time but just consider part of home, like steamed burgers, pizza or macaroni and cheese. A lush pyramid of dishes from all corners of the world, from all of our immigrant pasts. A little ritual, a pinch of celebration, a hearty spoonful of thanksgiving. Mix and serve.

Sources

Thanks to the many Connecticut restaurants and companies that contributed recipes, information and photos to this volume. Also thanks to Trena Lehman, for helping to test and adjust the dozens of traditional recipes. We couldn't have done it without her.

Bakke, Mary Sterling. *A Sampler of Lifestyles: Womanhood and Youth in Colonial Lyme*. New Haven, CT: The Advocate Press, 1976.

Beecher, Catharine. *Miss Beecher's Domestic Receipt Book*. New York: Harper and Brothers, 1846.

Beecher, Catharine, and Harriet Beecher Stowe. *The American Woman's Home*. New York: J.B. Ford and Co., 1869.

Beecher, Lyman. *Autobiography*. New York: Harper and Brothers, 1864.

Benes, Peter, and Jane Montague, eds. *Foodways in the Northeast*. Boston: Boston University, 1984.

Bidwell, Daniel Doane. "A Revolutionary Thanksgiving." *Connecticut Quarterly* 4 (January–December 1898).

Brown, Warren. *United Cakes of America*. New York: Stewart, Tabori and Chang, 2010.

Bunce, Louise. "The Home." *Connecticut Magazine* 6, no. 1 (January 1900).

Burros, Marian. "Election Cake: A Noble Tradition." *New York Times*, November 2, 1988, C12.

Child, Lydia M. *The American Frugal Housewife*. 12th ed. Project Gutenberg Online, September 18, 2004. E-text prepared by Audrey Longhurst, William Flis and Project Gutenberg.

Clark, George Larkin. *A History of Connecticut: Its People and Institutions*. New York: G.P. Putnam's Sons, 1914.

Connecticut Circle 4, no. 3 (March 1941); 5, no. 3 (March 1942): various articles.

Cronon, William. *Changes in the Land: Indians, Colonists, and the Ecology of New England*. New York: Hill and Wang, 1983.

Dojny, Brooke. *The New England Clam Shack Cookbook*. North Adams, MA: Storey Books, 2003.

———. *The New England Cookbook*. Boston: Harvard Common Press, 1999.

Donovan, Mary. *The Thirteen Colonies Cookbook*. New York: Praeger, 1975.

Earle, Alice Morse. *Home Life in Colonial Days*. Stockbridge, MA: Berkshire Traveler Press, 1898.

———. *Stage Coach and Tavern Days*. New York: Macmillan Company, 1915.

Einsel, Naiad, designer and illustrator. *Connecticut Cooks: Favorite Recipes from the Nutmeg State*. Connecticut: American Cancer Society, printed by R.R. Donnelley and Sons Company, 1982.

Emerson, Lucy. *The New England Cookery*. Montpelier, VT: Josiah Parks, 1808.

Faude, Wilson H. *Hidden History of Connecticut*. Charleston, SC: The History Press, 2010.

Fisher, MFK. *Consider the Oyster*. New York: North Point Press, 1988.

Flavor of New England. Introduced by Judith Ferguson. Surrey, UK: CLB International, 1989.

Friedman, Debra, and Jack Larkin. *Old Sturbridge Cook Book*. 3rd ed. Guilford, CT: Three Forks, 2009.

Glubok, Shirley, ed. *Home and Child Life in Colonial Days*. New York: Macmillan Company, 1969.

Hauptman, Laurence, and James Wherry. *The Pequots in Southern New England: The Rise and Fall of an American Indian Nation*. Norman: University of Oklahoma Press, 1990.

Hewitt, Jean. *The New York Times New England Heritage Cookbook*. New York: G.P. Putnam's Sons, 1977.

Hog River Journal. "The Way We Ate." Spring 2006.

Jacobs, Greta, and Jane Alexander. *The Bluefish Cookbook*. 6th ed. Guilford, CT: Globe Pequot Press, 2006.

Jacobsen, Rowan. *A Geography of Oysters*. New York: Bloomsbury, 2007.

Jenkin, James. "The Connecticut Oyster Industry." *Connecticut Circle* 4, no. 11 (November 1941): 10–11.

Kerr, Jean, and Spencer Smith. *Mystic Seafood*. Guilford, CT: Threeforks Publishing, 2007.

Lehman, Eric, and Amy Nawrocki. *A History of Connecticut Wine*. Charleston, SC: The History Press, 2011.

The Lymes' Heritage Cookbook. N.p.: Lyme Historical Society and Florence Griswold Museum, 1991.

Mark Twain Library Cook Book: A Treasury of Redding Recipes. Redding, CT: Mark Twain Library Association, 1971.

McPhee, John. *The Founding Fish*. New York: Farrar, Straus and Giroux, 2002.

Mead, Spencer Percival. *A History of the Town of Greenwich*. New York: Knickerbocker Press, 1911.

The Memorial History of Hartford County Connecticut, 1633–1884. Vol. 1. Edited by J. Hammond Trumbull. Boston: Edward L. Osgood Publisher, 1886.

Menta, John. *The Quinnipiac: Cultural Conflict in Southern New England*. New Haven, CT: Yale University Press, 2003.

Mercuri, Becky. *The Great American Hot Dog Book*. Charleston, SC: Gibbs Smith, 2007.

Monagan, Charles. *Connecticut Icons: 50 Symbols of the Nutmeg State*. Guilford, CT: Globe Pequot Press, 2007.

The New England Cook Book or Young Housekeeper's Guide. New Haven, CT: Hezekiah Howe and Company and Herrick and Noyes, 1836.

New Kirmesse Cook Book. Compiled by the First Church Mission Circle. Waterbury, CT, 1904.

Nylander, Jane. *Our Own Snug Fireside: Images of the New England Home, 1760–1860.* New York: Alfred A. Knopf, 1993.

O'Connor, Hyla. *The Early American Cookbook.* New York: Ridge Press, 1974.

Oppenneer, Betsy. *Celebration Breads: Recipes, Tales, and Traditions.* New York: Simon and Schuster, 2003.

Osborn, Norris Galpin. *History of Connecticut.* Vol. 2. New York: Stautes History Company, 1925.

Ozersky, Joh. *The Hamburger: A History.* New Haven, CT: Yale University Press, 2008.

Pepin, Jacques. *Jacques Pepin's Table.* San Francisco, CA: Soma Publishing, 1995.

Perl, Lila. *Red-Flannel Hash and Shoo-fly Pie: American Regional Foods and Festivals.* Cleveland, OH: World Publishing Company, 1965.

Peters, Samuel. *General History of Connecticut.* New York: D. Appleton and Company, 1877.

Pfeiffer, C. Boyd. *Shad Fishing.* New York: Crown Publishers, Inc., 1975.

Riccio, Anthony. *The Italian American Experience in New Haven.* Albany, NY: SUNY Press, 2006.

Simmons, Amelia. *American Cookery.* Fascimile of the 1st ed. New York: Oxford University Press, 1958.

Sixth Annual Report of the Secretary of the Connecticut Board of Agriculture, 1872–1873. Hartford, CT: Press of Case, Lockwood and Brainard, 1873.

Smith, Andrew. *Hamburger: A Global History.* London: Reaktion Books, 2008.

Stowe, Harriet Beecher. *Household Papers and Stories.* New York: AMS Press, 1967.

Twain, Mark. *Complete Works.* Edited by William Dean Howells. Kindle Edition, 2011.

Watson, Ben. *Cider Hard and Sweet: History, Traditions and Making Our Own.* Woodstock, VT: The Countryman Press, 2009.

Webster, A.L. *The Improved Housewife.* Hartford, CT, 1844.

Weeden, William B. *Economic and Social History of New England, 1620–1789.* Vol. 2. Boston: Riverside Press, 1891.

White, Jasper. *Lobster at Home.* New York: Scribner, 1998.

Works Projects Administration. *History of Milford Connecticut: 1639–1939.* Milford Tercentenary Committee, Inc. Bridgeport, CT: Bunworth, 1939.

Index

About the Authors

Eric D. Lehman and Amy Nawrocki are the coauthors of *A History of Connecticut Wine: Vineyard in Your Backyard*. Eric's essays, reviews and stories have appeared in dozens of journals and magazines. His books include *Bridgeport: Tales from the Park City*; *Hamden: Tales from the Sleeping Giant*; and *The Insider's Guide to Connecticut*. Amy is an award-winning poet whose three collections, *Potato Eaters*, *Nomad's End* and *Lune de Miel*, are available from Finishing Line Press. They teach English and creative writing at the University of Bridgeport and live in Hamden with their two cats.

Visit us at
www.historypress.net